RETIRE LIFE READY

RETIRE LIFE READY

Practical steps to build your wealth
and live your ideal retirement

JAMES WRIGLEY

WILEY

First published 2026 by John Wiley & Sons Australia, Ltd

© J&G Wrigley Pty Ltd 2026

The right of James Wrigley to be identified as the author of *Retire Life Ready* has been asserted in accordance with law.

ISBN: 978-1-394-33406-3

 A catalogue record for this book is available from the National Library of Australia

Registered Office
John Wiley & Sons Australia, Ltd. Level 4, 600 Bourke Street, Melbourne, VIC 3000, Australia

For details of our global editorial offices, customer services, and more information about Wiley products visit us at www.wiley.com.

Wiley also publishes its books in a variety of electronic formats and by print-on-demand. Some content that appears in standard print versions of this book may not be available in other formats.

Cover design by Alex Ross Creative
Cover Images: © Nataniil/Getty Images
Author photo: © Kristian Gehradte

Set in 12/16pts and Warnock Pro by Straive, Chennai, India.

Gabby, Thomas and Jack:
thanks for your support.
I love you.

CONTENTS

PREFACE

Hello!

My name is James and thank you so much for picking up this book.

I pinch myself every day that people choose me to help them manage one of the biggest transitions they will go through in their life. That transition being leaving behind what might have been a 30- or 40-year working life to, instead, live a life of leisure that we call *retirement*.

That transition often comes with equal parts excitement and fear, but with the right planning, you can tip the scales well in favour of excitement.

I'm a financial adviser, and as I begin writing this book, I've just turned 40. What would a 40-year-old know about retirement when, health permitting, I plan on working another 20 years or so? I often get similar questions to this from new clients I work with.

You are likely to retire once in your lifetime. At the age of 40, I have worked with and helped hundreds and hundreds of people retire. Together, with my colleagues, my business has helped thousands retire. I will, personally, work with hundreds more over the years to come.

I've seen the good, the bad and everything in between, and I hope to share some of that with you through this book.

In the last few years, hundreds of thousands of people have chosen to follow my social media pages where I regularly post short videos explaining lots of different things about personal finance. The interaction with those videos has put me in the rather unique position where I read hundreds and hundreds of comments every month from a wide range of Australians. So I have a great perspective of what people are going through, what they know and what they don't. Further, because of those videos, I get to speak with so many people about their own personal financial position and I see trends. I see what's worked and what hasn't at a scale not many other financial advisers in Australia have the opportunity to.

If you're anything like me, you're likely entering what might possibly be the most complicated money years of your life. As you hit a peak in your career and earnings, you may be juggling a demanding work schedule, raising a family, maybe supporting elderly parents, paying a mortgage and suddenly starting to worry whether you'll be okay in retirement.

Through this book, I hope to give you a framework you can apply to your own life so you can map out your own journey towards retirement so that you can retire life ready.

INTRODUCTION

You're likely going to be retired for a long time.

For someone who retires around the age of 60, you've got a pretty good chance of living into your 90s. That 60-year-old may spend another half of their life again (30 years) or a full one-third of their time on this earth not working — that's a lot of life. And it's a life I'd love to see you live to the fullest.

I like to call it retiring life ready, because this focuses less on what you are retiring *from* and more on what you are retiring *to*.

Your retirement means a life no longer limited by time because you have all the time in the world and, hopefully, if you follow what I'm about to take you through in this book, a life a little less limited by money than it may have been otherwise.

When I told my family I was going to write this book, it was over lunch for my 40th birthday. My aunty leaned over and said to me, 'James, make sure you tell everyone that unless they have money, retirement is boring'.

The financial outcomes of retirement is one thing, and the sooner you start planning for those financial outcomes, the better off you'll be, but there's the whole other side of what you want to do with your time when you eventually have a whole lot more of it once you stop working.

How to use this book

I'm going to ask you to complete a series of exercises to design your ideal retirement. I want you to write in the book, fill in the tables and worksheets, write in the margins, highlight the sections that are most important to you and use sticky tabs.

It's one thing to read a book from cover to cover, but you won't get the most out of this book until you really dive into it. I'd love to see how you use the book: share your workings with me on Instagram (@iamjameswrigley) and tag me in your posts.

You'll start by planning what you are going to do because what you plan on doing and when you plan on doing it will be a big indicator of the finances you'll need to support that life.

Once you've designed your ideal retirement, we'll take stock of where you're starting from. We'll work though what your ideal retirement might cost you and the level of assets you'll need to build to support the level of spending in retirement that you need. Finally, we'll explore all the various financial elements you can use to help you get there.

You'll then use these different elements to 'close the gap'. The gap being the difference between where you're starting from and where you're aspiring to end up, ready to retire life ready.

At the end of each chapter, you'll find 'Retire life ready steps'; it's important you complete each one before moving on to the next chapter.

While reading this book, completing the exercises and generally taking an interest in your finances is a step in the right direction, I can't stress enough the benefit of sitting down with a financial adviser and getting some personal advice on your situation. Even just taking the time to stop, think and talk about your situation with someone who has helped people like you in the past is incredibly valuable. I can't count the number of people I speak to and think 'if only I had have spoken with you just five years earlier' — please don't be one of those people. Get some financial help.

PART I
Start here and design your destination

This first section of the book is all about understanding where you are now and designing the retirement life you aspire to.

Rather than approaching retirement thinking, 'What retirement can I afford?' I'd love to see you designing the life you really aspire to. We'll then move on to helping you understand exactly where you are now financially, differentiating between the assets you have for your 'lifestyle' and those that will help you retire. We'll finish this part of the book by looking at a couple of different models to determine the level of assets you will require to support the retirement you're aspiring to.

You'll (hopefully) only retire once in your lifetime, and I want to see you living that life to the fullest.

CHAPTER 1

What are you retiring to?

Before we get into the *what* and the *how* of planning for your retirement, I want to introduce a different idea to you, a way of thinking about your future retirement that you may not have done before. I want you to open your thinking to *what you are retiring to*.

While retirement is the end of your working life, it's also the beginning of the next stage of your life.

According to the Australian Bureau of Statistics (ABS), in the 2022–23 financial year, there were 4.2 million people over the age of 45 who were retired: 2.3 million of them women and 1.9 million of them men. The average age at retirement (for all retirees) was 56.9, however, the average age people intend to retire is 65.4 years, with both of these ages trending upwards over time.

In my experience working in this space every day, a 'young' retirement these days (makes me sound old when I say phrases like that) is around 60. Lots of people in their 40s and 50s

I speak to talk about working until around 65, but I feel more people retire under 65 than over 65, and this is backed up by the ABS data. So keep in mind with your own retirement planning that you may not work as long as you think you will — perhaps by choice, perhaps forced upon you.

You'll probably spend more time in retirement than you think. Then, when you look at longevity, according to the ABS, a 60-year-old male is likely to live another 24 years while a female is likely to live another 27.

Goodbye routine, hello free time

During your working years, your life is governed by the routine of working life: Get up, sort out the kids, get them to school, get to work, work the day, home, dinner, clean-up, sleep, repeat. While many of us live that life, and it can feel never-ending at times, the routine gives our day structure, it gives us a purpose and reason to get out of bed in the morning. We need routine in our lives.

Holidays, during our working years, are an opportunity to stop, to break up the routine and do something different for a couple of weeks before going back to the routine of our day-to-day life.

But what happens when you stop working? What happens when the routine you've been so used to for all those years stops? What happens when all your time becomes leisure time? What will you do then? What will get you out of bed in the morning? What will give you purpose and belonging? What will make you feel fulfilled? What will be the break (that holidays once were) from endless leisure time?

While the idea of not having to be anywhere at any particular time, no-one expecting anything of you and every day being a

Sunday (I joke with all my retired clients), you really do need something to do — I've seen what happens when you don't.

In my job as a financial adviser, helping hundreds of people navigate the transition into retirement over the years, I've seen some people navigate this really well and others really struggle.

Client story: The value of staying connected

I'm reminded of one particular client, let's call him Bruce. Bruce really loved his work (as many people do), but he just worked too long. Bruce worked selling beer to pubs around Melbourne. I don't know how beer is sold to pubs in Melbourne now, but Bruce was from an era where you'd go door to door, one pub after another. Certainly, the number of customers he had grew smaller as the years went by, but he had his regulars. Bruce's wife would joke about trying to get him to retire but he wouldn't. Deep down I think Bruce's worries were twofold: I think he worried about not having enough money to retire on (which shouldn't have been a worry for him; more shortly), but I also think he had no idea of what to do if he stopped working. Many of his friends had already passed away, getting around a golf course would have been difficult, and if he stopped working, he wouldn't see all the people that he got to talk to in his work. Bruce loved a chat and to share a story.

On the financial front, Bruce and his wife had long paid off their house and saved up many hundreds of thousands of dollars in super and cash savings. Bruce and his wife were in the sweet spot where they didn't spend a large amount of money living, would qualify for a small part age pension and have plenty of their own money to supplement their retirement.

(continued)

While Bruce could have retired many years before he did, he just couldn't think of what else he would do if he didn't go to work every day. Bruce worked well into his late 70s and then just stopped. With nothing to do, no purpose, nothing to get him out of bed, his health deteriorated and, unfortunately, his retirement only lasted a couple of years before he passed. I'm no doctor, but I'm sure his working as long as he did, with nothing else to go to didn't help his health.

I don't want you to be like this.

The big retirement dreams

So what do people typically do once they retire? Some popular goals are:

- overseas travel
- domestic travel
- home renovations and repairs
- spending time with grandkids
- community engagement/volunteering.

Without a doubt, a long overseas holiday is at the very top of just about every retiree's wish list and, in my experience, it's rarely a one-off aspiration. People want to travel overseas annually for the first ten or so years of their retirement. For some people, they may have already started doing regular overseas holidays during their working lives. If the kids have grown up and left home or are working themselves, the mortgage has been paid off and super balances are looking healthy, I'm all for encouraging people to start travelling before they finish work. It's a whole lot easier to pay for when you have an income coming in. In many cases, I encourage them to go business class, because, why not?

What does it cost? For a couple, I say you'll be lucky to get change out of $30 000 for a four- or five-week overseas trip. Then, it depends if you are flying business or economy, what room you take on the cruise ship, if you're staying in an Airbnb or 5-star hotels and on it goes ...

Client story: Designing your own retirement

I have one client, let's call her Jane, who has travelled consistently since the day she retired. A hike was one of the first things Jane did when she finished up work and from there she got the bug. Jane finds new friends everywhere, and every trip results in new buddies that she does other trips with.

Jane would pride herself on how light she could pack, often travelling for weeks on end (well into her 60s mind you) with just a backpack. She jokes with me now, more than ten years into her retirement, that she can't quite pack like she used to. Jane spends six to nine months a year travelling around Australia and the world, and she wouldn't have it any other way. Finding time for our four-monthly check-in is always a challenge because she has adventures planned 18 months in advance, but we make it work.

On the financial front, Jane travels at incredibly low cost and that $30 000 allowance for the couple I mentioned previously would cover Jane's annual travels — she loves staying in backpackers' hostels.

One other thing Jane has done that not many other clients have is purchased time share — and quite a bit of it. Jane has

(continued)

> the money to buy it so that's not a worry, but what it does is force her to keep going away and taking her friends with her because she doesn't want to see the time shares go to waste. It works really well for her lifestyle.

What's on most retirement wish lists?

Most retirees gear up for the overseas holiday; that's the big thing they are looking forward to. Also towards the top of that list for most people heading into retirement is to do those jobs around the house that you didn't quite find the time to do while you were working. Perhaps it's repainting, maybe it's updating the bathroom or kitchen now that you have a little more time to plan.

From a financial planning perspective, we really like to have an idea about what's on the home reno list and what it might cost. If you go dropping $150 000 on a new kitchen and a couple of bathrooms in the first 12 months of your retirement, and haven't planned for it, it could mean your retirement savings run out a whole lot earlier than is comfortable.

Part of this home renovation work can be setting your house up for the next stage of your life. I'm not talking ramps and grab handles, but if you're like Jane who spends six to nine months a year away from her home, you need that set up. During COVID, Jane re-did a lot of her garden, making it much more low-maintenance and installing irrigation, and fixed up the kitchen and bathroom. Jane made the decision that she wasn't going to downsize from her house, so she needed to spend a bit of money bringing it up to standard for the next 15 to 20 years, but also making her garden a whole lot less work to come back to after a holiday. Clients tell me there is nothing worse than coming home from five weeks away on some amazing holiday only to have to spend the next two weeks fixing up the garden.

Lots of people buy a new caravan and car, the combination of which has become frightfully more expensive in the last five years FYI, and head off for months on end exploring Australia. The new car-and-caravan combo used to cost around $100000, after you allowed for trade-in of your current car, but that combo is now more commonly closer to $200000. Then, if you push up the size and weight of the van, this reduces the number of cars that can tow such a weight. Then you need some after-market additions because the standard Land Cruiser won't quite cut it. If you're in this world, some of these numbers won't surprise you. If you're considering it, start calculating your numbers now. You need to add this to your retirement planning numbers.

Are your retirement dreams similar to this or do you have something different? Whatever they are, write them down in the table here. Have you considered what those goals may cost you?

Retirement dream purchase/project	Estimated cost
	$
	$
	$
	$

But what about the day to day?

Now, I want you to think a little deeper about what you are going to do in retirement. Think past the overseas holiday and those household jobs that you haven't found the time for. Those things will come and go very quickly. Ask yourself questions like: Who are you going to socialise with? What's going to make you feel connected, give you purpose and meaning in your life?

What may surprise you is that a number of people find themselves going back to work. Particularly if they retired younger. The reasons vary as to why people find themselves going back to work, but can include the following:

- Perhaps the retirement may not have been their own choosing. They may have lost their job for some reason, and, because they were around the age of 60, thought they would give retirement a go only to find they weren't retiring on their own terms, so went back to work for a few years.

- On numerous occasions I've had clients take voluntary redundancies. They work for a big corporate, a new leader comes in and does a restructure and some voluntary redundancies are offered. The money looks attractive, they are around the age of 60, so think, 'Why not?' and take a package. After they've taken the overseas holiday and painted the house, they get bored so go back to work.

- The other common scenario I see is a career change. They've done the same thing for the last 40 years, maybe with different employers but much the same job. They are sick of it, retire and then work part time in a completely different field. The part-time work is often on their terms and fits in around holidays and looking after the grandkids.

When you could access your super at age 55, I encountered a number of people who would 'try' retirement. It's a lot less common now that you can't access your superannuation until you are 60.

So back to the day to day. Things like the following can keep you active, develop social circles in retirement and help you feel like you belong:

- family
- grandchildren
- community groups
- probus clubs for retired people
- men's sheds
- university of the third age (U3A)
- church groups
- sporting clubs.

Often my happiest retired clients are those who are involved in the running of these groups. The retired accountant is often the treasurer of the golf club, that kind of thing. These clubs help give retirement a degree of structure. There's committee meetings that are held on a regular basis, work of some variety that is required between the meetings and people who are relying on them. It's this kind of thing that helps break up the leisure time I mentioned earlier.

Another big thing that I want you to think about is where you are going to live. For most retirees (they never say it out loud, but I can pick it up from their body language) it can be overwhelming thinking about living somewhere other than where they currently do. For others, that's part of the adventure — they plan to sell their house, buy something small that doesn't require much maintenance so that they can lock-up and leave, then spend half the year or more out seeing the world.

I would encourage you to think about moving home in your earlier retirement years. The more active (earlier) part of your retirement is a much easier time for you to deal with moving house than leaving it to later in your retirement.

The three main phases of retirement

It's well documented across a number of sources, and I experience it directly with my clients, that you'll usually have three main phases of your retirement years. Those three phases of your retirement are the:

1. active years

2. sedentary years

3. frail years.

The active years

The active years are typically between the ages of 60 through to early/mid-70s.

You'll have the fitness to cope with the adventures that come with the early part of retirement. For those who aspire to travel the world, you'll often be doing a lot of it during this period. It's not uncommon for people, as mentioned earlier, to build annual overseas holidays into financial plans for at least the first ten years of retirement.

Your primary concern during this period is your next adventure. When you aren't travelling, you'll be playing lots of golf or diving head first into other hobbies, and you're generally able to get out and about without too many issues.

Those with grandchildren are in a unique position to spoil them with time and attention, as all of a sudden a retired grandparent has all the time in the world. We often hear about research that highlights how positive parent–child relationships are central to emotional and social development, but we rarely see studies into the importance of grandparent–grandchild connections. When regularly involved in day-to-day activities, grandparents can actually help reduce household stress as they are the perfect playtime companion. The ability to engage in creative, imaginative play isn't hindered by work commitments or a looming deadline, which is often the case for parents. Many grandparents talk about how much they love this time.

This period of time often coincides with your peak spending years in retirement. For those with renovation plans and grand overseas adventures, you want to factor that into your financial plans.

The sedentary years

The sedentary years typically fall between the early/mid-70s to early 80s.

I hear it all the time from clients that by this age they have seen all the things they want to see around the world. The long flight time from Australia to anywhere else really takes its toll (even if you are flying business class) and they've had enough of it. It's usually those with family living overseas who continue pushing through the long flight hours.

Another factor to consider is that travel insurance becomes difficult to obtain once you're over the age of 80, and many people over this age avoid America in particular as the costs associated with their health system mean they don't want to risk ending up in hospital over there.

In these years your activities tend to slow down. There's a little less golf, there's a little less travelling, there's a little less of everything. During this time, superannuation draw-down rates increase (more on this in Chapter 7), so you can find yourself in a situation where the minimum pension drawdown from your superannuation is more than what you actually spend. If you aren't spending it travelling, it just builds up in your bank accounts, and it's not uncommon for me to see grandparents using this extra money to help their children or grandchildren. Grandparents paying school fees for their grandchildren is a whole lot more common than you might think.

Most people assume their spending will reduce during this period when compared with the earlier active years, and they are right, but it's not quite what they expect. What I see happening in practice is, instead of your spending continuing upwards due to inflation, your spending might flatline.

So instead of spending $80 000 one year on your day-to-day living needs (outside of holidays and other one-off events) and then spending $82 000 (because everything is a little more expensive next year due to insurance) the next year, spending tends to stay flat at $80 000 for a period of time. Given you are less active, the money doesn't have to go so far. Inflation erodes the spending power, but as you aren't doing so much, the money stretches further. Prior to the inflationary period post-COVID, it wasn't uncommon for me to see clients have that spending flatline for five or six years before they needed anything more. It's not quite the same length of time today, but this flat lining still does play out to a degree.

The frail years

The frail years typically extend from the early/mid-80s onwards.

In the later years of retirement, your spending on leisure drops off a lot. Travelling and discretionary spending decrease the most during this time, and are often replaced with increased medical costs, home care costs and sometimes residential aged care (more on this in Chapter 11).

If aged care isn't needed, this phase may involve a downsize. As I mentioned on page 12, my preference is to see you to do this earlier in retirement when you are more easily able to cope with it. The major concern for you and your family is quality of life during this stage, so continuing some community engagement, spending time with family and friends, and engaging in other hobbies is incredibly important.

There will be increased reliance on your family during this stage, and often a renewed focus on the division of one's estate. This may be prompted by your financial adviser, by you or perhaps your children. Either way it's important that those in your life know your wishes, know where to find key documents and who to contact (accountant, financial adviser, lawyer etc.). More on this in Chapter 10.

Retire life ready steps

Now that you've made it through Chapter 1, your task is to think about what you are going to do in your retirement. This is more than just imagining your dream holiday destination; this is an opportunity for you to think about designing the life you want. We'll get into the numbers and details later, but for now, think about what you want from your life.

Filling in the following will give you a good start:

What are your top three travel destinations?

1. _____

2. _____

3. _____

What needs fixing/repairing around the house?

_____

_____

Would you consider moving house? If so, where would you move and how would it affect your day-to-day cost of living?

_____

_____

_____

How are you going to maintain connection? What are your friends and family doing? What can you do to be involved with them?

_____

_____

_____

What community groups do you want to know more about?

_____

_____

_____

If money was no object, what would you do?

_____

_____

_____

That final question gets you thinking about the bigger picture. Money may, ultimately, be a limiting factor in real life, but don't let it be for that question. Dream big — this is your dream retirement you're building.

CHAPTER 2
Where
are you now?

You may have a clear idea of what you want your retirement to look like — your big dreams, how you want to spend your days, and what will get you out of bed each day — but before we get too excited, we need to work out what that retirement is going to cost you and how you're going to build the assets to fund it. You need to take stock of where you are now.

For some, this may be a painful exercise, but it's important to acknowledge and take responsibility for the position you are starting from and move forward. Time spent dwelling on why you are where you are is wasted time.

There are four basic numbers that you need to know to have a starting point upon which you can build. We'll also come back to these numbers and the workings of how you arrived at them at different points throughout this book, so keep your workings handy.

Those numbers are what you:

1. earn

2. spend

3. own

4. owe.

Let's take a look at each one in turn.

1. What you earn

What you earn is the sum total of all the after-tax income that hits your bank account over a year. This is what you earn from work; what your partner earns; what you might collect in bonuses, rent, dividends, profit distribution — anything.

If you don't know what you expect to earn over the year, how can you possibly make any plans for the future around your money?

Income type	Amount (after tax)	Freq.	Annual total
Salary Individual 1	$		$
Salary Individual 2	$		$
Bonus	$		$
Profit share	$		$
Rent (investment property)	$		$
Interest (bank accounts or term deposits)	$		$
Dividends (shares)	$		$
		TOTAL	$

2. What you spend

Do you know what you spend? Maybe budget tracking is your personal Olympic sport, perhaps it's not something you focus on, but it's time to work it out. What you spend will vary from week to week and month to month, but it's important you have a handle on what you expect to spend over a set period. It's impossible to know to the exact dollar what you might spend this coming year, but you can look back at what you spent last year, and that's a great place to start.

This exercise will be tedious but important because it's how we take steps towards building your ideal retired life. It's really important you know where you are at so you can really start to move forward.

In this section, you need to not only include expenses like mortgage, groceries, utilities, insurance, school fees etc., but also any regular investing you might be doing at the moment. Perhaps you're already adding a little extra to your super, or you have an investment property that you have to contribute some money towards.

Home maintenance

Expense	Amount	Freq.	Total	Continue in retirement?
Mortgage	$		$	
Rent	$		$	
Council rates	$		$	

(continued)

Expense	Amount	Freq.	Total	Continue in retirement?
Water	$		$	
Electricity and gas	$		$	
Home and contents insurance	$		$	
Strata/ body corporate	$		$	
Gardener/ cleaner/ pool etc.	$		$	
	$		$	
	$		$	
	$		$	
	$		$	
	$		$	
	$		$	
	$		$	
	$		$	
	$		$	
	$		$	
	$		$	
	$		$	
		TOTAL		

Living costs

Expense	Amount	Freq.	Total	Continue in retirement?
Essential living costs				
Food and groceries	$		$	
Clothing	$		$	
Utilities				
Mobile phone	$		$	
Internet	$		$	
Education				
School fees	$		$	
Other education costs	$		$	
Entertainment				
Eating out/ takeaway	$		$	
Netflix/ Spotify/ Disney+ and other streaming services	$		$	
Health				
Private health insurance	$		$	
Doctors	$		$	
Dental	$		$	

(continued)

Expense	Amount	Freq.	Total	Continue in retirement?
Medication	$			
Insurance				
Life insurance, income protection etc. (paid personally)	$			
Other	$			
Pets				
Vet costs	$			
Pet food/pet insurance	$			
Transport (for all cars, boats etc.)				
Registration	$			
Insurance	$			
Servicing	$			
Road tolls	$			
New tyres	$			
Fuel	$			
Bus/train/ tram passes	$			
Travel				
Holidays	$			
Weekends away	$			

Expense	Amount	Freq.	Total	Continue in retirement?
Other				
Hair/beauty	$		$	
Nanny/ childcare	$		$	
Gym/yoga/ Pilates etc.	$		$	
Club memberships	$		$	
Birthday gifts	$		$	
Christmas gifts	$		$	
	$		$	
	$		$	
	$		$	
	$		$	
		TOTAL	$	

Loans and repayments

Expense	Amount	Freq.	Total	Continue in retirement?
Outstanding credit card repayments**	$		$	
Car loans	$		$	
Personal loans	$		$	

(continued)

Expense	Amount	Freq.	Total	Continue in retirement?
Tax debt	$		$	
Investment loans	$		$	
	$		$	
	$		$	
	$		$	
	$		$	
		TOTAL	$	

** Only include an amount here if you carry an outstanding balance that isn't repaid each month.

Saving and investing

Type	Amount	Freq.	Total	Continue in retirement?
Saving	$		$	
Investing	$		$	
Super contributions	$		$	
	$		$	
	$		$	
	$		$	
	$		$	
		TOTAL	$	

Add it all up, the totals from each of these spending tables. Now, once you know these two numbers, do this simple calculation:

What you earn
– what you spend, save and invest
= what you have left to do something with

Total household income	$
Less Total annual spending	$
TOTAL	$

When you look at your spending, if your number seems high, it probably is. But, also remember, that you can only cut your expenses so far. At the most basic level, you need to pay for food, clothing and shelter, and that's going to cost you something. On the other hand, there is no limit to how much money someone can earn. Sure, certain occupations pay more than others, but you could change occupations, study, start a business etc., and increase what you earn.

3. What you own

What you earn and what you spend looks at your cash flow, essentially what cash comes into your house and what goes out. Now I want you to work out what you own, otherwise known as your assets. This includes things like your house, cars, boat/caravan, holiday house, cash in the bank, shares, super, investment property and business interests. In the earlier sections you wrote down what you earn from these assets, now you're looking at the value of the asset itself. Add up everything that you own at their current values.

Lifestyle assets

Asset	Value
Home	$
Vehicles	$
Caravan/boat/motorbikes	$
Holiday home	$
TOTAL	$

Nest egg assets

Asset	Value
Cash/term deposit/offset account	$
Combined super balances	$
Investment property	$
Shares/managed funds	$
Business value	$
TOTAL	$

4. What you owe

What you owe, otherwise known as your liabilities or debts, includes everything that you owe to someone else or, more commonly, a bank. This could be a home mortgage, investment property debt, car loan, personal loan, credit card, student debt, or business loans.

Debt

Liability	Amount
Home loan	$
Investment loan (property or shares)	$
Car, boat, caravan loan	$
Holiday home	$
Superannuation debt	$
Business debt	$
TOTAL	$

Putting the numbers together

Now that you've worked out what you have left after deducting your spending from what you earn (i.e. what you earn – what you spend, save and invest = what you have left to do something with), hopefully what you earn is more than what you spend, and the difference can be allocated towards your future. I say *hopefully* because the reality for many people is that their equation is reversed (what they spend is more than what they earn).

If you have discovered that you are spending more than you are earning, then this book is going to give you the tools to reverse that so you can retire life ready.

If these two numbers are the wrong way around for you, you need to take a hard look at where you are spending money. I'm a big advocate for spending on things that bring you the most joy, but you also need to be ruthless in cutting back on the things that don't. Even if what you earn versus what you spend is the right way around for you, this is still a good opportunity to re-evaluate whether you are spending money on things that mean something to you or whether you can cut them out.

It happens to the best of us

A few years back, we moved between a few rental properties in a short space of time while our house was being built. While moving from one rental to another, I arranged contents insurance for our new rental house but was still paying for content insurance for the old one for a brief crossover period while we moved. After we settled into the new rental, I forgot to cancel the old contents insurance. A few months later I went through this exercise of working out where our money was going only to find I was paying contents insurance for a property we had stopped renting a number of months earlier. Oops.

Hopefully, what you own is worth more than what you owe, that is the total value of all your assets is worth more than your liabilities. The difference between these two numbers is known as your net worth.

If what you owe is more than what you own, all is not lost. You might have some work ahead of you and some tough decisions about whether certain assets are helping you or holding you back. The good news is that by working through this book and completing the exercises, you will gain the skills, the tools and the confidence to restructure your finances so your expenses don't outpace your earnings, and you can do something about that deficit so you retire life ready.

Now that you have these four numbers (what you earn, spend, own and owe), you're in a better position of understanding your finances than most. You also have the starting point from which you can start building your retirement plans.

Working out your nest egg assets

There's one final piece of number crunching I want you to do here, and it focuses on the numbers you came up with for the assets that you own as well as the debts that you owe (flip back to pages 28 and 29 to find this). The final piece I want to introduce you to here is the idea of 'net nest egg assets'. You see, not all your assets will help you retire — it's your nest egg assets that will.

When I first meet with new clients, we talk about these concepts I'm explaining to you, and some people will take great pride in telling me what their net asset position is. They might say to me they are worth $2 million or $5 million or $7 million or more, but I feel like I'm bursting their bubble when I go on to say that, because most of that asset position they are so proud of is tied up in the value of their own home and other lifestyle assets, they aren't in the position to retire any time soon.

Let me help you understand the difference here. You'll notice with the list of assets you put together on page 28, I had you break them up into two groups: lifestyle assets and nest egg assets. This was on purpose.

Lifestyle assets

Your lifestyle assets are things like your home, your holiday house, your car/boat/caravan/motorbike. They are great things to have and often bring a lot of joy to your life, but they do not help you retire. For instance, the more expensive the home you choose to live in is, the further you may be from being able to retire. A more expensive home comes with more expensive upkeep (insurance, council rates, etc.), which means you need more investment assets to provide the income to support that expensive home, let alone the mortgage you need to repay so that you can own it before you retire.

Nest egg assets

The second type of asset is your nest egg assets. These are things like your cash savings or term deposits, superannuation balances, investment property, share portfolio or business interests you intend on selling. These are the assets you will, ultimately, use to help fund your retirement. They are assets that, when invested appropriately, will generate you an income that you can use to support your retirement. Your home doesn't generate you an income; it only costs you money.

Calculating your nest egg assets

Put the list of lifestyle assets to the side. From your list of nest egg assets (page 28), I now want you to subtract the total value of what you owe (page 29). Subtract all of it, the whole number you worked out at step 4. It doesn't matter what that borrowed money was used for, all that matters now is that you need to repay it at some point in the future.

Nest egg assets
– what you owe
= net nest egg assets

Assets	Value
Total nest egg assets	$
Less Liabilities	
Total debts	$
Equals	
NET NEST EGG ASSETS	$

It's not uncommon for the net nest egg assets number to be negative, and the younger you are, the more likely it is that it will be in the negative. Once you hit your 40s and early 50s, this number is more likely to be around zero and it builds from there.

Before you start to worry, know that this number can build from negative to zero to a big positive number very quickly as there are two forces working to push it in the right direction:

1. Over time, you pay down your debts through ordinary loan repayments, which reduces the 'what you owe' number.

2. At the same time, you add to your super balance, the value of your savings or investments grows, and so your nest egg assets number grows. It's not uncommon to see a swing of $1 million or more over a ten-year period.

Knowledge is power

This has been quite an active chapter, and it's okay if you find yourself revisiting the activities in this chapter a number of times.

You should now have a handle on where you stand financially *today*. You should know what money comes into your house, what goes out, what you own and what you owe. Most importantly, you should now understand that it's not your total asset position that will ultimately help you retire, but your nest egg assets.

Retire life ready steps

Now that you've worked out where you're starting from and what your plan for retirement might be, can you identify anything this early on that you need to work on? Now is your chance to write down three steps you can take right now to start on the path for financial freedom in retirement. Perhaps you feel some financial advice would make things clearer. You might want to reassess how you are contributing to your super (more advice on this in Chapter 7), or are you thinking about whether the assets you have are working for you in the right way? Whatever it is (and it doesn't have to be big), write down three things you can do right now.

1. _____

2. _____

3. _____

I'd also like you to think about how often you are going to check in on the calculations you did in this chapter to find out what you earn, spend, own and owe. This can change over the course of your working life, so don't set and forget this exercise. You might even pair it with your tax return so you deal with all your finances once a year and get a solid picture of where you are at.

I'm planning to revisit my financial situation every _____ months/years. I will do this by _____.

Now that you're really clear on what your dream retirement looks like and the baseline you are starting from, let's look at ensuring your financial set-up will support that dream post-working life. To ensure you can retire life ready, your goal will be to build this net nest egg number. In the next chapters, we'll look at how big that number should be and what you can do to grow it.

CHAPTER 3
How much do you need in retirement?

Let's think about your retirement. Back in Chapter 1, when I asked you to visualise your retirement with no financial limitations, what did that look like? If you were to achieve that dream, how much do you think you would need? Would $1 million be enough? Could you get by with $500 000? Or maybe your dream requires multiple millions?

Thinking about what retirement might mean for you can be the most confusing part. There's so much that has been written about this topic that it's hard to know what is right for you.

A group called ASFA publish a quarterly report called the 'ASFA Retirement Standard', which is interesting reading as you head towards retirement. Their quarterly report gives you a breakdown of how much people (either a single person or a couple) spend in retirement, living what they describe as either a comfortable or modest retirement. Not only do they give you a headline number, for example, $73 875 for a couple to live a comfortable retirement (as at March 2025), they give you a breakdown of where that money is spent. They also convert that annual spending number into a lump sum you will need at age 67 to support that lifestyle, heavily subsidised by the age pension over time and assuming you spend all of your lump sum over the remainder of your life.

This sounds like the magic answer most retirees are looking for to the question of how much they are going to spend and how much money they need to have saved up. While every time ASFA release a new quarterly report the spending numbers increase, my experience is that those numbers are on the low side, and what ASFA consider comfortable, isn't the comfortable I see people aspiring to in retirement. As just one example, their definition of a comfortable retirement when it comes to travel is an annual domestic trip to visit family and one overseas trip every seven years.

My point here is that you should take a step back from the guides and the averages that you might have read about and instead focus on *you*. This is your retirement that you are designing, no-one else's. So what matters for someone else or what an average might be doesn't matter. Don't waste your time comparing yourself to others. We're going to use the numbers you worked out in Chapter 2 to build what you need for your dream retirement.

Where to start

My preferred place to start is with how much you plan on spending in retirement. What will be your annual spending? Once you've worked out your spending number, then we can work out how much you'll need invested to support that.

Some people leave the planning a little too late. They work out what they can spend based on the amount they retire with. This isn't ideal because it's not reflective of the retired life you *want* to live, and can lead to you compromising on your retirement plans. If you have the time ahead of you, start with your desired spending in mind and then work from there.

In the first chapter of this book, I asked you to think about what you are retiring to, what was going to get you out of bed each day, what was going to give you purpose. Now you need to try and put some numbers around that. It may be as simple as you wanting to continue spending and living as you do now while you are working, or perhaps there are some changes you'd like to make. Maybe you've been sacrificing some lifestyle activities so you can diligently save and invest for a more comfortable retirement, or perhaps you're thinking the opposite, and maybe you've travelled extensively either for work or pleasure so you might be looking at spending less in retirement than you currently do now.

Your spending position

If at all possible, I like to see people in the same spending position in retirement as they are now, with perhaps a little extra available so they can have a bit more fun than their current work schedule allows. I make the point of considering your *spending* position because this is not about replacing your income form work with the same income from investments — it's unlikely you'll need that much.

Right now you earn an income, pay tax, pay your bills, pay your mortgage, save for retirement, live etc. Some of those things that you spend your money on today (such as your mortgage) will stop either before you retire or when you retire, so you don't need to account for them in your annual retirement spending number.

Some of those things you spend your money on now will continue, and it's the things that continue that are of most importance here.

Let's use some of what you worked out in Chapter 2 to work out your spending position for retirement.

Step 1: Work out what expenses will stop

Go through the exercise in Chapter 2, where you worked out what you spend, and identify everything that will stop by the time you retire. This will be things like mortgage repayments, school fees and education costs, nannies/childcare, income protection, car loans, investment property loans, savings, investing and super contributions.

Ideally by the time you have retired, you'll have paid off all your debt. Even debt on an investment property isn't something you want to carry into retirement as what typically happens is any rent you do earn just goes to expenses and paying the loan back — it doesn't leave you anything to spend.

There's also no need to budget for further saving or investing once you are retired. At that stage, you want to use the income from investments to live off, not to save.

What will stop by retirement?	Annual amount
Mortgage repayments	$
School fees	$
Life and income protection insurance	$
Car loan	$

What will stop by retirement?	Annual amount
Investment property mortgage	$
Regular savings or investing	$
Additional super contributions	$
	$
	$
	$
TOTAL	$

Step 2: Work out what's left

Add up the total of all that you identified in step 1 and subtract it from the total spending number you identified in Chapter 2. After you've subtracted all those things that will stop after you've stopped working, you'll be left with a number representative of what costs you to run your house and your life — what I referred to earlier as your spending position.

Total spending before retirement
– expenses that will stop after retirement
= your spending position

Step 3: Add in any new expenses

While you've identified expenses that are likely to stop once you retire, you also need to think about the additional expenses you may incur in order to live the ideal retirement you visualised.

If there are a few extra things you identified when you were designing your ideal retirement in Chapter 1 that you aren't currently doing, you need to add an allowance for those activities. By this I mean the extra regular activities, not the lump sum renovation costs or the new car or caravan — we'll add those into the mix later. Do you plan to get out and explore a little more than you currently do? If so, you need to factor that in. Are you planning on taking up an expensive hobby? If so, now's the time to include it in your budget.

Total annual spending	$
Less What stops by retirement	$
Add extra retirement activities	
Holidays	
Hobbies	
Exercise classes	
Equals	
Spending position	$

Giving and offering support

Now is also a good time to also start thinking about whether there is anyone in your life who you will need or want to help financially.

Perhaps you have a desire to help your children with a deposit for their first home. This is an incredibly common aspiration for lots of clients I work with. They see the current cost of housing and wonder how their children are ever going to afford to buy a house. So we build into their retirement plan a level of assets to support themselves as well as an amount that will be gifted (or perhaps loaned for asset protection purposes) to their children to buy a house. Perhaps there is someone in your life who will require your ongoing support. If you need to contribute to their living needs as long as you and they are alive, then we need to include that annual cost into the retirement spending number.

When it comes to children, I see some parents being over supportive (giving far too much towards the purchase of a house, for example). In these situations, I explain to the retiring parents that the best thing they can do for the financial stability of their children is be financially secure themselves. The last thing you want to do is be too generous with your children, only to not have enough money to support yourself, then need your children to support you financially later in life. It's not a great position for anyone to find themselves in. It means not only will things be tough for you financially but you may also be making things tough for your children financially too.

Your spending number

So, after all of this, we arrive at your retirement spending number. How much will you need to live your dream retirement life? This number will be unique to you and the lifestyle you want to lead. I have some clients I work with who are comfortable living off $50 000 to $60 000 a year (despite ASFA's definition of a comfortable retirement), and I have others who spend $250 000 a year. The difference between those two extremes most commonly comes down to:

- what they each did during their working lives
- what they earned during that time and the lifestyle they were used to living during those years

- how generous they plan on being with their children and extended family through retirement.

What your spending number is and how that aligns with the life you want to live will be unique to you.

The rule of 20x

Now that you have a figure that represents how much you want to spend in retirement, we need to convert that number into a level of assets you'll work towards. By doing this, we will make that annual spending number a reality.

For this exercise, I want to introduce you to the idea of the rule of 20x. Quite simply, multiply the retirement spending number you worked out on page 40 by 20. This figure will give you a guide to the level of assets you'll need to accumulate in order to support your desired retirement income. Importantly, this figure represents *net nest egg assets*, as we discussed in Chapter 2, and it doesn't include your lifestyle assets.

The rule of 20x is based on you earning a long-term average return on your retirement savings of 7 to 8 per cent, which is a fairly common long-term return number for most balanced super funds. It's certainly not an unachievable number. This means you need to invest your money, and not too conservatively either if you are to earn 7 to 8 per cent in long-term average returns (more on retirement investing later in Chapter 14).

If you can earn 7 to 8 per cent as long-term return on your money, it will allow you to spend 5 per cent of your capital each year (being the first part of your earnings) and leave the remaining 2 to 3 per cent invested to continue growing your retirement savings, so that your spending can keep up with inflation over time.

If we put some numbers to this, let's say you start with $1.5 million, and you earn 7 per cent per annum on your money and spend 5 per cent each year. It looks like this:

Year	Net nest egg assets at beginning of year	Earnings	Spending	Remainder earnings
1	$1 500 000.00	$105 000.00	$75 000.00	$30 000.00
2	$1 530 000.00	$107 100.00	$76 500.00	$30 600.00
3	$1 560 600.00	$109 242.00	$78 030.00	$31 212.00
4	$1 591 812.00	$111 426.84	$79 590.60	$31 836.24
5	$1 623 648.24	$113 655.38	$81 182.41	$32 472.96

You'll notice that the starting balance continues to grow (being the previous year's starting balance plus the remainder earnings), as does the earnings and spending. While the numbers are going up because of inflation, this is really just keeping your spending power intact over time, and you end up with the retirement asset projection that so many people aspire to that looks like figure 3.1.

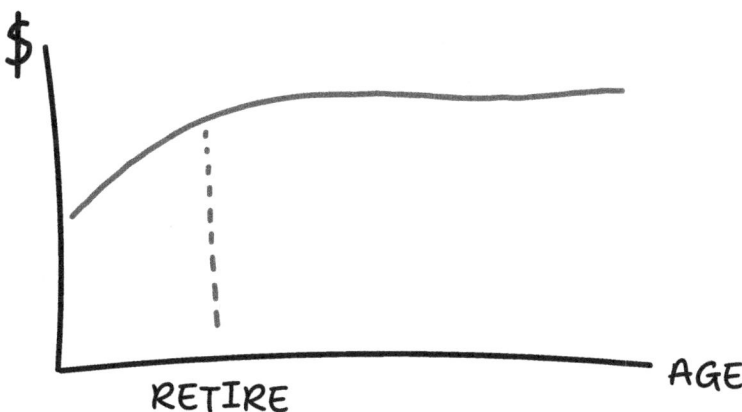

Figure 3.1: Maintaining spending power over time: The retirement savings curve most people aspire to

The spending power of your assets remains steady throughout your retirement, leaving you to pass that nest egg on as inheritance, in addition to your home and any other lifestyle assets you own.

Here are some examples of desired spending and assets you'd need using the 20x rule.

Desired annual spend	Assets using 20x rule
$60 000	$1 200 000
$80 000	$1 600 000
$120 000	$2 400 000
$180 000	$3 600 000

These numbers assume you are fully self-funding your retirement and you don't get any age pension. That's not always realistic because, at the lower retirement spending numbers (around $60 000, for example), you could structure your finances in such a way so most of your spending is covered by the age pension with only a small top-up from your own savings and investments — so needing $1 200 000 isn't necessary. For higher retirement spending numbers, you can't rely on the age pension quite so much. (We'll look more closely at the age pension in Chapter 9.)

Remember, this is just a guide to see if you are in the ballpark and give you something to work towards. It's possible to retire with assets much less than what the 20x rule suggests, which means it is likely you will use up some of your retirement savings over time. Some people are more than happy with that and others aren't.

The other big thing you'll need to factor into this is inflation. The rule of 20x allows for inflation on your retirement spending over time, but it doesn't allow for inflation between today and when you do retire. Say you're targeting retirement spending of $120 000 a year but you don't intend to retire for another ten years. You'll need to increase the $120 000 for ten years' worth of inflation and then use the 20x rule.

So $120 000 per annum now, inflated at 3 per cent per annum for ten years becomes $161 270. Then using the 20x rule, your asset requirement becomes $3 225 400 (instead of $2 400 000 if you didn't account for inflation over the next ten years).

Here's the maths for how you can account for inflation:

$$\text{SPENDING} \times (1 + \text{INFLATION RATE})^n$$
$$n = \text{YEARS TO RETIREMENT}$$

$$e.g. \ 120{,}000 \times (1 + 3\%)^{10}$$
$$= \$161{,}270 \ (\text{ROUNDED})$$

In Chapter 4, we'll cover working out the gap between where you are now and where you need to be to retire life ready.

RETURNING TO THE RULE OF 20X

Before we finish up with the rule of 20x, there are a couple of other really important things to understand. The rule of 20x is essentially based on you earning a consistent return of 7 or 8 per cent (one that doesn't vary from year to year) on your retirement savings, and the assumption that you'll only ever spend 5 per cent of your retirement capital each year, both of which aren't realistic.

It's not realistic to assume that you will only ever spend 5 per cent of your capital each year — something will pop up that you could never have accounted for and this is perfectly normal. It won't (within reason) derail your retirement as the rule of 20x ensures you have plenty of money to cover your retirement spending. You just don't want to be over spending every year, which could lead to problems.

You will also never see identical returns year after year like this rule assumes. Long-term average returns are exactly that — an average. To get a long-term average return of 7 to 8 per cent, you'll have a random distribution of negative returns and positive returns, both small and large in each direction, and possibly even some zeros for good measure. This distribution of returns over time is known as *sequencing of returns*.

Here are two examples of sequences of returns that, starting with the same $1 000 000, have the same average return of 7 per cent over the ten years, but would result in different retirement savings balances over time. In keeping with the rule of 20x, in each year 5 per cent of the starting balance is spent.

There isn't a huge difference between the balances after the ten years (only about $1900), but there are big differences during the ten years. After year 4, for example, Portfolio 1 is around $111 000 in front of Portfolio 2 before Portfolio 2 catches up through to year ten.

Two different portfolios will behave differently based on what they are invested in. This exercise isn't to highlight one being better than the other, rather, it points out the different journey you may have over ten years, even though both portfolios have the same average return.

Year	Annual % return Portfolio 1	Amount	Annual % return Portfolio 2	Amount
Start		$1000000		$1000000
1	10	$1050000	6	$1010000
2	7	$1071000	18	$1141300
3	12	$1145970	-2	$1061409
4	11	$1214728.2	9	$1103865.36
5	-4	$1105402.66	6	$1114904.01
6	7	$1127510.72	8	$1148351.13
7	6	$1138785.82	7	$1171318.16
8	-1	$1070458.67	-3	$1077612.7
9	15	$1177504.54	9	$1120717.21
10	7	$1201054.63	12	$1199167.42

Then, finally, in order to access 5 per cent of your retirement savings each year, the mix of investments you hold those savings in matters a lot. I'll discuss investing for retirement in Chapter 5, but in order for the rule of 20x to work best, your assets need to be liquid (i.e. you need to be able to redeem parts of your investment over time, such as cash, term deposits and shares).

Take an investment property, for example. While you may earn an average return on that property of 7 to 8 per cent per annum, only a very small portion of the return you earn will be the rental income (the cash you can spend). If the income you earn from an investment is low, you need to be able to sell part of your investment over time to make up the difference between the income you earn and what you need to spend. You can't sell off small parts of the property to make up the shortfall in your income — you either own the whole property or you don't.

If you rely solely on a residential investment property to fund your retirement (without selling it), you cannot rely on the rule of 20x as you won't earn enough rental income for it to work.

The 4 per cent rule

Similar to the rule of 20x, the 4 per cent rule is another way of looking at the level of assets you might require to safely provide for your retirement. The FIRE (Financial Independence Retire Early) community typically use this as their rule of thumb. It's another guide to what may be a safe draw-down rate (the rate at which you draw on your retirement savings), allowing you to spend at the level you desire for your retirement and minimise the likelihood that you will run out of money during your retirement.

For the 4 per cent rule, take your desired retirement spending level that you worked out on page 40, then divide that by 4 per cent. This will give you a nest egg number that you need to be aiming for. It results in a slightly higher number than the 20x rule calculates.

Remember when I explained the rule of 20x on page 42? I explained that the rule of 20x was based on you spending 5 per cent of your capital (or net nest egg assets) each year. Well, using the rule of 20x, you could either divide your desired annual spending by 5 per cent or multiply it by 20x, the net nest egg assets number you need is the same. I just find multiplying something by 20x easier maths to do in my head than dividing something by 5 per cent.

Then the last of the geek out on the maths: When you divide the same number (desired annual spend) by a smaller percentage (4 per cent for the 4 per cent rule, instead of 5 per cent for the rule of 20x), the answer is a bigger number — a bigger net nest egg balance.

Following are some example asset levels you'd need using the 4 per cent rule:

Desired annual spend	Assets needed using 4 per cent rule
$60 000	$1 500 000
$80 000	$2 000 000
$120 000	$3 000 000
$180 000	$4 500 000

The 4 per cent rule is a more conservative way of calculating what you might need to fund your retirement. When I say conservative in this context, I mean the 4 per cent rule says you need a higher net nest egg balance to fund your retirement than the rule of 20x does. The higher your net nest egg balance, the more 'safety' you are building into your retirement savings. This means that you are less likely to run out of money over time.

The younger the age you want to retire by (think mid-50s and younger), the more I'd advise using the 4 per cent rule because you have a longer period of time you need to fund without working, and hence, you're aiming for a bigger number. If you're targeting a more average retirement age, say of 60 to 65, then the rule of 20x is likely to be sufficient.

While some of this can feel quite dry, and let's be honest, it's not nearly as much fun calculating your yearly spend as it is actually spending it, it's important to remember that we're aiming to grow your wealth so you can live your dream life and retire life ready, and that is pretty exciting.

What about the one-offs?

Whether you're using the rule of 20x or the 4 per cent rule, or some other means of calculating the level of assets you might need to fund the retirement income you desire, don't forget about those one-off expenses you had planned.

On top of the resulting assets from either the rule of 20x or the 4 per cent rule, you need to add the one-off expenses, such as the home renovations, the new car or caravan, and gifts to children or others in your life (discussed on page 9). Those lump sum numbers need to be added on top.

Assets to fund retirement
+ one-off expenses or gifts
= total assets you need

There, you've done it. You've worked out the assets you need to be targeting to retire life ready.

What's the gap?

In Chapter 2, you worked out where you are now using the net nest egg assets method. On pages 42–49, you worked out where you need to be using either the rule of 20x or the 4 per cent rule. Now to round out this chapter, you're going to work out the gap between where you are now and where you need to be so we can then start bridging that gap. So let's work it out.

How much you need in retirement
– net nest egg assets
= the gap

As I briefly touched on back on page 32, when working out either where you are now or how much you need in retirement, you can't include any of your lifestyle assets, such as the value of your house, your holiday house, your car, boat or caravan — these are all nice to haves and are quite possibly things you plan on using a lot when you are retired. They don't help you retire.

If, on the other hand, you are planning on selling your holiday house, downsizing your home (not just in size but in value) or selling some of the 'toys', then you can subtract the value of the sale or downsize or the value of other lifestyle assets you plan on selling from your gap.

If the gap seems like a big number, don't worry too much. The power of time and compound returns, which we will explore in detail in the next section, will help you close that gap.

On the other hand, if there isn't any gap or, better yet, you're in surplus — congratulations. This gives you options.

- You can stop working if you want to. You're now working because you want to and not because you have to.

- There's the option of setting yourself an even higher target. Perhaps there are some things you'd really love to be able to do in retirement that you were holding back from when you were designing your dream retirement.

- You could also be generous with your giving. No matter who you are giving to, a gift with warm hands is far better than one with cold. Your gift recipient will be even more grateful.

Closing the gap

In order to retire life ready, you need to close the gap between where you are today and the net nest egg assets you require to fund your ideal retirement. There are so many ways to slice and dice preparing for retirement over time. Part III of this book is dedicated to the idea of closing the gap.

There are many books on the topic (this one included), podcasts, videos, a whole ocean of content out there on the internet designed to help you. Some of it does an incredibly good job of it; some of it makes it all far too confusing.

People think they need to map out these overly complex plans to help them build their wealth over time and put them in a position so they can retire. Quite often, the perceived need for complexity stems from a lack of understanding of where they need to get to in the first place — but that's not you anymore, you know exactly where you need to get to.

I prefer to try and keep things as simple as possible when it comes to closing the gap. In Australia, there are two key requirements to a comfortable retirement.

1. Own your own home.

2. Have enough money in other assets to provide an income to support that retirement, with the backup of the age pension system.

We'll revisit this topic in more detail in Part III, but it's so important for you to be able to live the life you want in retirement that you do the work to close the gap.

Understand the building blocks

Before we rush off to the building stage and mapping out plans for how you will close your gap, it's important that you have an understanding of the Australian finance landscape, which we will look at in Part II.

Once you understand the various elements that will come together to help you retire life ready, you'll feel far more in control of why you are doing different things and how they will put you in the best position for your retirement.

Retire life ready steps

The rule of 20x and the 4 per cent rule are two calculations that allow you to determine how much you'll need in retirement. Ask yourself:

Which one of these calculations is going to be most useful for your planning? _____

Using the examples on page 42 and page 48, roughly calculate the figures that each rule returns for you.

Rule of 20x:
Spending number _____ x 20 = _____ assets to fund retirement

4 per cent rule:
Spending number _____ ÷ 4% = _____ assets to fund retirement

What one-off expenses can you foresee in the next five years?

1. _____ $_____ (approximately)

2. _____ $_____ (approximately)

3. _____ $_____ (approximately)

What about the next ten years?

1. _____ $_____ (approximately)

2. _____ $_____ (approximately)

How much will you factor in for those one-off expenses post-retirement?

Part I has been about getting you to take a realistic look at your current position and where you might like to be financially when you retire life ready. The next part of this book will look at the ways you can use your super, tax and other levers to set yourself up for a financially free retirement.

PART II

The building blocks to your destination

Through this second part of the book, I'm going to explain a range of different financial elements and topics. Each on their own is important, but also think of them as building blocks. You are unlikely to be dealing with any one of these elements in isolation.

Navigating your financial life as an adult will require juggling a number of these elements. The combination in which you use them, as well as the order, will differ from one person to the next. There's no right or wrong path here, just your path.

CHAPTER 4
Debt as a friend and foe

It's near impossible to go through your adult life without borrowing money. Buying a house, buying a car, having a credit card: we are bombarded in day-to-day life with offers of 'credit' and 'equity'. If you're to retire life ready, all your debt needs to go. All of it by the time you retire.

There's a time and place for debt, but that's not during your retirement. Used wisely, debt is an incredibly powerful tool that can really boost your ability to build wealth over time, but get too carried away with it and it's like a house of cards that will come crashing down at the slightest breeze. Used incorrectly, debt is a handbrake on your finances and can be the reason why you struggle to reach your full financial potential.

Good debt vs bad debt

Let me get this out first, I hate the phrase 'good debt vs bad debt'. Debt is debt. It all needs to go before you can really retire life ready. Let me explain.

Regardless of what the debt (borrowed money) was used for, it will come with some type of commitment from you to make a regular repayment. That might just be the interest or it could be the principal and the interest. Either way, there is a repayment that needs to be made and that repayment is a drag on your retirement cash flow. If you need to fund your lifestyle and your debt repayments in retirement, you'll need even more assets to retire life ready.

Good debt

Good debt refers to money that you have borrowed to purchase an investment asset, such as an investment property or some shares. Where you've used money to purchase an income-producing asset, then the tax rules allow you to claim the interest you pay on that borrowed money as an expense against your income. Where the interest cost of the borrowed money is more than the income you earn from the investment you have purchased, you can use the excess interest expense as a deduction against any other income you earn — this is what's called negative gearing. I'll cover negative gearing in more detail in Chapter 6.

This so called *good* debt will result in you getting a tax refund, at most (if you earn over $190 000) of 47 cents for every dollar in interest you pay, which means that you are still out of pocket 53 cents for every dollar in interest you incur.

For example, let's say you earn over $190 000, which puts you in the top marginal tax rate of 47 per cent, and you borrowed $800 000 for an investment property at an interest rate of 6 per cent. The interest on the borrowed money would cost you $48 000 per annum. The best case scenario is that you can claim that full $48 000 interest cost as an expense in your tax return so you may receive a tax refund of $22 560 ($48 000 × 47%).

You are still out of pocket $25 440 ($48 000 interest cost *less* $22 560 tax refund).

If the investment you have purchased isn't growing by at least the amount you are out of pocket each year, you are going backwards financially at quite a rapid pace — doesn't sound so good, does it?

I've had so many people say to me they are going to use equity in their home to buy another investment property when they are fewer than five years out from retiring. When I question them on why they are doing that, they say: 'to build their wealth for retirement'. But that extra debt just puts them further away from being able to retire unless they turn around and sell the property only a few years after purchasing it.

The new property purchase will result in a negative drain on their cash flow. Most of the time, the rental income they receive from the new investment property isn't enough to cover the loan repayments and all the other outgoings associated with the property. Where the cash flow is short, they have to make up that shortfall from other sources, often their employment income or other investment income. At best, any rent they receive will just go to making loan repayments — it might not cost them anything out of pocket, but the property also doesn't provide any rental income they can spend to help fund their retirement while debt remains on the property.

When you play this scenario out a little further, their only option is to turn around and sell the property a few years after purchasing it. Not a great outcome when you factor in the costs to acquire the property and sell only a short time later. I find, for most people, they are better off using those last few years to pay down their debt (not take on more), if they haven't already done so, and squeeze a few more dollars into superannuation.

Bad debt

Bad debt is the phrase used to describe money you have borrowed to purchase an asset or a thing where you can't claim the interest cost of the borrowed money as an expense. Within the bad debt space, there are bad debts and there are *extra* bad debts.

The not-so-bad debt is money you have borrowed to purchase your own home. Yes, you pay that loan and the interest back with after-tax money — it's not terribly tax efficient, but owning your own home is the number one thing you can do to secure a comfortable retirement for yourself. So, as far as bad debt goes, it's not such a bad debt.

The other not-so-bad, bad debt is student HECS/HELP debt. This is a debt to the Australian Government you incur by studying a higher education (uni or TAFE) course. Now, hopefully you put those studies to use and secured a great job working in an industry you otherwise wouldn't have been able to. Why is this debt not so bad? You don't pay interest on this money, you pay indexing (which is just interest by another name). On 1 June each year, any outstanding HECS/HELP debt is increased by the prevailing indexing (interest) rate, which is near enough to the going rate of inflation.

The long-held wisdom is that the indexing on your HECS/HELP debt will be the lowest interest rate debt you will ever have in your life, so you are better off paying other debts back first before you ever worry about your government student debt. This was true, until the sky-high indexing that occurred during the post-COVID run up in inflation, which saw student debts increase by over 7 per cent in one year. At the time of writing this book, inflation had come back down again to around 3 per cent, in which case I feel that the lowest-interest-debt argument is back to holding true again.

The bad, bad debt is where you have borrowed money for consumption or to buy assets that typically go down in value. The two classics are running up credit card debt and living beyond your means, such as paying for all or part of a holiday you can't actually afford for the 'experience' you will provide your family, only to then spend the next 18 months repaying said holiday at a cost of 20 per cent interest … sound familiar to anyone? The other being buying a car you can't afford, but you can afford the loan repayments (or so you think), so fool yourself into thinking you can afford the car.

As a bit of an aside, I'm a car guy, but I really like Scott Pape's (of Barefoot Investor fame) idea that you should only buy cars/ boats/toys etc. to a maximum value of half your annual after-tax income and, where possible, pay cash for said items. Once your mortgage is paid off and your super and investments are humming, then I think you can splash out a bit more — or at least that's my plan anyway.

If you are feeling overwhelmed by your debts, reach out to your bank, a financial adviser or mortgage broker who may be able to help you put a plan together to tackle it. Sometimes you just need some help. Being overwhelmed by debt doesn't mean you can't turn it around — and maybe that means bringing in professional help.

Paying off your debts

Remember, we are trying to build *net nest egg assets* here that will, ultimately, leave you in a position to be able to retire. The equation for net nest egg assets was nest egg assets less all your debts. So, you can either build your assets or pay off your debts — or both — to increase your net nest egg number.

If you still have a mortgage, I'd like you now to work out how long it will take you to repay your mortgage at the rate you are currently paying it. Will it be repaid by the time you retire or do you have some work to do on this front?

For this, you will need to use a mortgage repayment calculator. My favourite one is Mortgage Monster at https://mortgage.monster.

The Mortgage Monster calculator allows you to put in the details of your remaining outstanding loan, interest rate, repayment frequency, and, if you have money in an offset account, you can enter that too. Then, adjust the slider on the remaining 'term' category to how many more years you have between now and when you plan to retire.

Is the resulting repayment more or less than what you currently repay?

If it's less, congratulations — you are on track to being mortgage free before you retire. If it's more, well, you've got some work to do to ensure you become mortgage free before you plan to retire. The good news is I'm going to show you exactly how to go about closing the gap.

A lot of households are carrying more than just a home loan: there might be car loans, credit cards, personal loans, ATO debts … the list could go on and on. If that's the reality in your household, it's time to get serious about repaying those debts. The longer they hang around, the slower your progress to retirement will be.

Client story: Aligning your reality with your expectations

I once did some work with a couple who had plans to retire at a particular age. They had two children they were putting through school but were very short-sighted with their financials. They could be really good savers when they wanted to, but would happily spend all their savings on a family holiday. I'm all for the family holiday and making memories and absolutely that should be something factored into their financial plans.

The problem was they were only making minimum loan repayments, and at the rate they were making repayments, they wouldn't pay off their mortgage until they were almost 70. They wanted to retire by the time they were 60. If they were still carrying the home loan past age 60, they couldn't retire. So, we had to have a conversation about their priorities. Were more family holidays and working another ten years okay, or did they want to trim down on the holidays and finish work a little earlier? There's no right answer, there's just *their* answer.

In what order should you repay your debts?

If you do have multiple different debts to repay, you absolutely need to factor in how you are going to repay them by the time you retire. You've really got two choices:

1. Repay them with cash flow, through regular monthly or fortnightly repayments.

2. Sell assets, possibly pay some capital gains tax (more on this in Chapter 5) and use the proceeds to repay the debt.

The second option is a very common element of the retirement plans we put together for clients when we are doing proper paid financial advice engagements. We'll often have clients selling shares or property, at the right time, to repay debt and, more appropriately, set themselves up for retirement. We manage the sale and things like superannuation contributions to manage the tax outcomes as best we can.

I want you to list all of your debts in the following table, as you'll need to come up with a plan to repay them. If you need more space than this you can download the template from my website (jameswrigley.com.au). You'll need to look at your bank website or app for things like the outstanding amount on your home loan, interest rates and minimum repayment details; same for your credit card, car/boat/caravan loan and any buy-now-pay-later debts you might have. If you're making more than the minimum repayment on any of your debts, note it next to the table below, but for the sake of the exercise, only record the minimum repayment amount.

Debt description	Interest rate %	Outstanding amount	Minimum repayment $
		$	$
		$	$
		$	$
		$	$
		$	$
		$	$
		$	$

When it comes to repaying your debts with cash flow, the maths would say to repay the debts as follows:

1. Make minimum repayments across all your debts.

2. Direct any extra cash you have for repaying debt to the bad (non-tax-deductible) debt first. Then direct your extra cash to the loan with the highest interest rate first, until that is repaid. Then tackle the next highest interest rate and the next highest interest rate after that and so on.

3. Once that bad debt has all been repaid, focus on the good (tax-deductible debt). If you have multiple good debts, focus on the highest interest rate first until that is gone before moving to the next highest interest rate.

The reason you want to repay the bad, non-tax-deductible debt first is because you don't get any tax deduction for the interest cost of that borrowed money. You have to pay the principal repayment and the interest cost with after-tax money. On the other hand, with tax-deductible debt, you pay the principal repayment with after-tax money, but the interest charge with pre-tax money (because you can claim the interest as a tax deduction). Essentially, the tax-deductible debt is cheaper for you, so you only want to pay that off after you've paid your more expensive, non-deductible debt.

Snowball your debts

While the mathematical preference is for you to repay your debt in the order of highest to lowest interest rate, non-deductible debt first, then move on to your tax-deductible debts, most people will feel like they are making more progress by repaying their debts in the order of smallest to largest.

If you start with the smallest debt first, it can feel a lot easier to repay it, which makes you feel like you are making better progress, which, in turn, motivates you to pay off more debt. This strategy is known as 'snowballing' your debt repayments.

The snowball (being the money you are putting towards the debt repayment) gets bigger as you knock off one debt and push that repayment into the next debt.

Let's have a look at your existing debt using the snowball method. You've already compiled a list of your debts in the table on page 29. Now, reorder that debt in the table here starting from the smallest bad debt to the largest bad debt, then the smallest good debt to the largest good debt.

Debt description	Outstanding	Minimum repayment
Bad debt		
	$	$
	$	$
	$	$
	$	$
Good debt		
	$	$
	$	$
	$	$
	$	$

Now that you have a clear picture of how you could use the snowball method to tackle your debt, think about which method will work best for you. For those who feel like they don't know where to start, I suggest using the snowball method — you'll feel like you are making better progress.

Using debt to your advantage

Debt used in appropriate levels, at the right time, in your asset-building stage, can provide a tremendous boost to your net nest egg assets at retirement.

The premise is quite simple: borrowing money for investment purposes (purchasing things like property or shares) allows you to purchase more or bigger investments than you would have otherwise been able to purchase on your own without the borrowed money. The bigger purchase, growing at whatever growth rate your investment grows at, results in more dollars in your back pocket. Let me explain with some numbers.

Value of investment	Return in year one	Investment value at end of year one	Dollar value return
$100 000	10%	$110 000	$10 000
$500 000	10%	$550 000	$50 000

You can see both investments had the same 10 per cent return, but the bigger $500 000 investment earned more ($50 000) than the smaller $100 000 investment did ($10 000). Now if the difference between the $100 000 investment and the $500 000 was $400 000 you borrowed from the bank, you could (ignoring taxes for simplicity) sell your investment for $550 000, repay the bank $400 000 and keep the $150 000: your original $100 000 investment + your $50 000 return.

You'd have some interest to pay on the borrowed money, but, even allowing for that, you're far better off in this example than you would have been only investing $100 000.

Now, in reality, the bank will want to be paid some interest for the money you borrowed so that should be factored into the return, as should capital gains taxes on the sale of your asset, but you get the idea. Borrowing money for investment purposes can help you earn greater returns than you otherwise may have been able to earn on your own.

While borrowing money can magnify your gains if things go well and you earn some good returns, it will also magnify your losses if things go badly and you have negative returns. Let's look at an example.

Value of investment	Return percentage	Investment value at end of year one	Total losses
$100 000	–10 per cent	$90 000	$10 000
$500 000	–10 per cent	$450 000	$50 000

In this scenario, the return is negative 10 per cent, instead of positive 10 per cent in the first example. When you're just investing your own $100 000, the value of your investment drops by 10 per cent down to $90 000. But, if you had borrowed $400 000 to make a $500 000 investment that then drops by 10 per cent, the bank still wants their $400 000 back, which only leaves you with $50 000. Plus you still need to pay the bank's interest bill too. Not a great outcome, but this highlights one of the major risks you need to consider when you use borrowed money for investing.

The final thing you need to be aware of when borrowing money for investment purposes is the impact it can have on your cash flow. When you borrow money from the bank, the bank will want you to make repayments on that loan, likely at least monthly. The bank doesn't care what's happening with your investment, they want their monthly repayments and you'll need to come up with the cash to make those repayments. For most people, those repayments are more than the income the investment generates leaving them in a negative cash flow position and possibly a negative-geared position as I explained on page 58.

As I said earlier in this chapter, the last five years of your working life is not the time to be taking on more debt, it's time for repaying what you have — particularly your home loan. Target retiring debt free through a combination of regular repayments and the sale of investments if you have to.

Retire life ready steps

Looking at the debts you listed on page 29, categorise them into good debts and bad debts. Using either the snowball or repaying bad debts first method, calculate how long it will take you to pay off those debts.

You can use the calculator on my website (jameswrigley.com.au) to work out how long it will take you to pay off each debt.

Your mortgage is one of the biggest debts you will likely have across your lifetime. Looking at the calculations you have just done, where will you be with your mortgage when you are ready to retire? $_____

If you were to be mortgage free by the time you retired, how much extra would you need to start paying fortnightly/monthly/yearly? $_____

For some people, this may be achievable, for others, the number might be a bit more out of reach. The good news is that, in the next chapters, we are going to dive into other tools and assets you have access to that will enable you to still build wealth for the future, so you can live your dream retirement.

CHAPTER 5

The secret sauce to an epic retirement through investing

In this chapter, we'll cover why investing is so important for growing your retirement wealth and how you can get started.

Investing without an understanding of how the taxation system works is a bit like you only hearing one side of a conversation. The two are somewhat intertwined, and the success (or otherwise) of your investing efforts will have an influence on how much tax you have to pay. The more of the return you get to keep because you've managed your tax situation well, the better. Ultimately, it's the after-tax return that will determine how successful your investing activities have been.

If hearing words like 'after-tax return' starts to give you a headache, don't worry. We'll cover tax and how to manage it in Chapter 6.

The sooner you start investing, the better. Time is your friend when it comes to investing. The more time you have for your investments to build towards your desired net nest egg balance, the less you need to contribute on a regular basis, and also the less risk you need to take with your investing.

Let's say you need to build $1 million, and for this example, you're starting at zero. You have no investments at all, and your first instalment is your first step towards the $1 million you need to build. If we assume you earn an annual return of 8 per cent on your investment, and we ignored taxes and inflation to keep things simple, the following table shows you how much you would need to contribute on a monthly basis, and how many years you would need to do that in order to build an investment portfolio of $1 million.

Number of years	Monthly deposit required to save $1 million	Total of regular deposits	Interest earned
40	$286.45	$137 496.11	$862 503.89
35	$435.94	$183 095.69	$816 904.31
30	$670.98	$241 552.47	$758 447.53
25	$1051.50	$315 448.66	$684 551.34
20	$1697.73	$407 456.17	$592 543.83
15	$2889.85	$520 173.75	$479 826.25
10	$5466.09	$655 931.13	$344 068.87
5	$13 609.73	$816 583.66	$183 416.34

Note: Any slight variations are caused by rounding decimal places.

Now, $1 million in 40 years from now isn't going to buy you anywhere near what $1 million would buy you today because of the impacts of inflation. But the point of this exercise is that, if you had started investing just $286 per month 35 years ago, you'd only need to keep going for another five years (for a total of 40 years) to get to your million-dollar target. That's a whole lot easier than finding $13 609 per month if you were starting from zero and needed to build your $1 million in five years.

The best time to start investing was 40 years ago; the second best time is today.

Please don't wait until you have paid off your mortgage before you take investing for your retirement seriously. As this exercise shows you, a small amount invested for a long period of time gets you the results. If you wait 25 to 30 years until your mortgage has been paid off, that's 25 to 30 years' worth of compound investment returns you've missed out on.

Compounding returns on your investments over an extended period of time will generally outweigh paying off your mortgage faster. Well, at least that's what the maths would say, the nuance being your own unique circumstance and preferences — that's where personal financial advice can become incredibly beneficial.

The power of compound returns

You may already understand the idea of compound returns, but it's important I spend a bit of time explaining it anyway as it's one of the building blocks of investing. With time, it's the compound returns that will really get your net nest egg assets moving and your money working hard for you.

You'll no doubt understand the idea of putting some money in a bank account and earning interest on that money. If you had $10000 in a bank account and earned 5 per cent interest on your account for the year (ignoring tax for simplicity), you would have $10500 at the end of the year.

Now, for the second year, your original $10000 earns another $500 in interest (5 per cent interest on the $10000 for the second year) *plus* you'll also earn 5 per cent interest on the $500 interest you earned last year. Which is another $25.

So, in year one you earned $500 interest, in year two you earned $525 interest, and that interest just keeps compounding year on year. Here's what it looks like if we keep this going for 10 years.

Year	Deposit	Interest	Ending balance
1	$10000	$500.00	$10500.00
2		$525.00	$11025.00
3		$551.25	$11576.25
4		$578.81	$12155.06
5		$607.75	$12762.82
6		$638.14	$13400.96
7		$670.05	$14071.00
8		$703.55	$14774.55
9		$738.73	$15513.28
10		$775.66	$16288.95

You'll see in year ten, you've earned $775.66 in interest. You're not only earning interest on the original deposit, but also the interest earned in the previous year.

Earning interest on your interest is one of the building blocks for investing. Do it for long enough and you end up with a balance that looks like figure 5.1.

Figure 5.1: Compounding in action: How reinvested returns accelerate your investment growth

All the magic with compound growth happens at the end. In the beginning, it's boring. Not much happens and the growth in your investment or account balance is slow. In this early stage, the biggest influence on your investment balance is the money you are able to add to it, not the investment returns. People worry so much about chasing the best possible investment returns. Sure they matter, but they matter very little in the beginning when the biggest influence on your investment balance is your ability to contribute towards the investment.

As time goes on, the investment returns will make a bigger and bigger difference and the benefit of compound returns will start to take over. At this point, it's time in the investment that matters more than the rate of your contributions (unless you are contributing very big sums of money).

It all clicked for me when someone explained compound returns like this:

You think by delaying starting a year, it's just the beginning you are giving up. Not much happens in the first year, so it's not much of a big deal. But what, in fact, you are giving up is another year at the end, where all the magic happens (see figure 5.2).

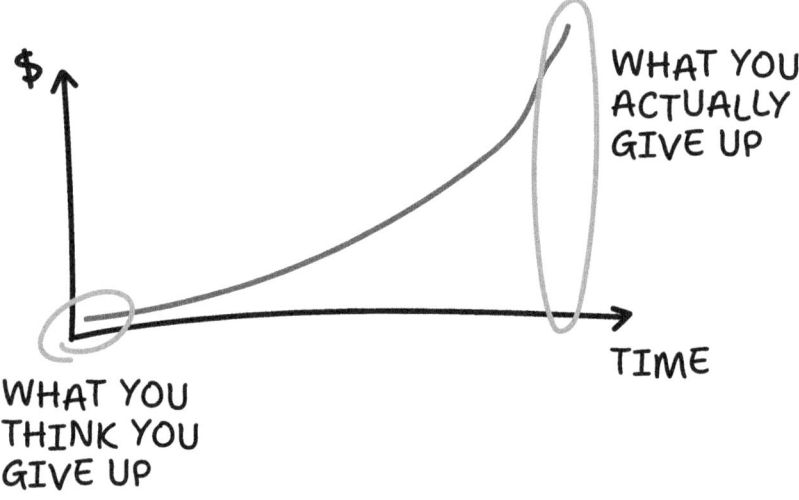

Figure 5.2: The real cost of delaying: Why skipping the first year means losing the most powerful one

Investment types

Let's look at the four broad asset types available to you as an investor. While there are many other types of investments and derivatives of the four I'm about to explain, you don't really need them. Remember, we want to try and keep things simple as you build towards your net nest egg number and your financial freedom in retirement.

Within each of these four investment types, there are various subtypes or ways of accessing each investment. The four broad asset types are:

1. cash

2. bonds

3. shares

4. property.

More recently, crypto and block chain–backed assets have become mainstream. Crypto and block chain are a whole other world of investing and we won't be delving into them in this book.

Let's take a look at the four asset types.

1. Cash

Cash can be the physical folding stuff or deposits in a bank account. Keeping too much physical cash on hand isn't a great idea for a number of reasons, not least of all, in the event it gets stolen. It also doesn't earn you any return if it's not at least in a bank account earning interest.

Cash in the bank is government guaranteed up to $250 000 per person per bank. At the time of writing this book, there were very reasonable interest rates on offer from various banks, particularly considering that, prior to COVID, interest rates on bank accounts where practically zero. The rates on offer at present are especially good given there is no risk to your money (because of the government guarantee), and you have instant access to it as it's a cash account.

Too much of a good thing isn't great, and the same applies for cash savings. Even at 5 per cent interest on your savings account, once you allow for tax on the interest you earn at, say, 30 per cent if you're earning up to $135 000, your after-tax interest rate becomes 3.5 per cent, and with inflation running at about that same rate, your real return (the return you earn after allowing for inflation) is practically zero. So your cash might be safe, but it's not actually earning you a return when you allow for tax and inflation.

ONLINE SAVINGS ACCOUNTS

You'll need some cash in an ordinary transaction account for living and spending day to day — this account isn't likely to pay you any interest at all. Some banks offer higher rates of interest for their online savings accounts. You often can't spend the money directly from the online savings account, instead, you have to transfer it back to the transaction account for spending.

Some banks make you jump through endless hoops, like depositing a certain amount into your savings account each month, making a certain number of transactions on a linked transaction account or not withdrawing from your savings account, to get some bonus interest on their online savings accounts. Others are just happy to have your money on deposit and will give you the good interest rate without needing to do ten star jumps while singing the alphabet backwards.

TERM DEPOSITS

With a term deposit, you lock your money away for a set term, perhaps three, six, 12 months or more. Typically, the longer the duration of your term deposit, the higher the rate of interest you will receive, this being compensation for you not having instant access to the cash. However, term deposit rates also take into account the bank's outlook for interest rates. If the economy is slowing and there is an expectation that interest rates will start to reduce, term deposit rates offered by the bank will reflect this. A longer-term deposit (say, 12 months) may offer a lower interest rate than a shorter term deposit (say, three months). This is because the bank expects interest rates to reduce over the next 12 months, and they don't want to be stuck having to pay you a higher rate of interest after rates have dropped.

OFFSET ACCOUNTS

Finally, if you have a mortgage, you may have an offset account. An offset account is an account linked to your home loan. The balance of your offset account is subtracted from the outstanding balance of your home loan, and the bank only charges you interest on the difference, rather than the whole balance of your home loan (see figure 5.3).

Figure 5.3: Offset accounts in action: How you can cut the amount of interest you are paying

Offset accounts can be amazing and, if used correctly, help you save years in repaying your home loan. As with many things, if not used properly, they can end up costing you in the long run. If you have a large sum of money sitting in an offset account, it can be very easy to fall into the trap of thinking you can afford to spend because you have so much money sitting in the bank.

If you do have a mortgage and you have cash savings sitting anywhere other than in an offset against your home loan, move it. Money you have sitting in a savings account earns you interest, you pay tax on that interest and keep what's left. Money in an offset account doesn't earn you interest, it saves you interest. You will save more interest on an offset account than you will get to keep after you've paid tax on the interest from your savings account.

Let's look at an example showing the after-tax interest earned on $10 000 in a savings account earning 5.5 per cent compared with that same $10 000 in a offset account against your mortgage, where your mortgage rate is 6.1 per cent. The interest earned on the savings account leaves you with $374 after you've been taxed (assuming 30% marginal tax rate + 2% Medicare) on the $550 interest earned. Now look at how that money works for you in an offset account: The $10 000 will save you $610 in interest on your mortgage (being $10 000 multiplied by your mortgage interest rate of 6.1%). There's no tax to pay on the interest saved so you are comparing $374 in interest earned (after tax) with $610 interest saved on your mortgage. Clearly the offset account is the better option.

When you look at it this way, the offset gives you a better long-term outcome than the savings account. Even if the interest on your loan is tax deductible, you are still better off putting the cash in offset than you are putting it in savings, if you don't have a loan on your own home you can offset (see figure 5.4).

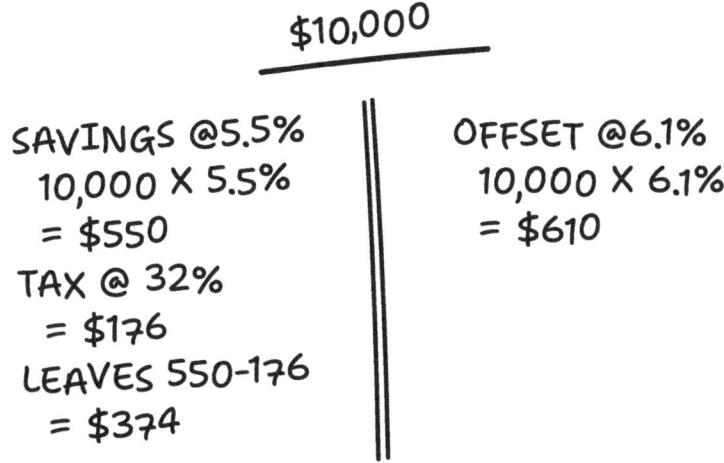

$10,000

SAVINGS @5.5%	OFFSET @6.1%
10,000 X 5.5%	10,000 X 6.1%
= $550	= $610
TAX @ 32%	
= $176	
LEAVES 550-176	
= $374	

Figure 5.4: Offset vs savings account: a side-by-side comparison of real interest saved

Ideally, the only money you should have sitting in cash is what you have earmarked for spending in the next three to four years or is being used to offset/repay debt. Outside of that, you're going backwards by keeping too much money sitting in cash.

2. Bonds

Fixed-interest assets or bonds are typically loans you make to governments or businesses in exchange for an interest payment and return of your capital investment at the end of the bond's duration.

For example, you might purchase an Australian Government bond, which is a loan you make to the Australian Government, usually for up to ten years, in return for a series of quarterly interest payments they will make for the duration of the bond.

Bonds trade on markets in a similar fashion to shares, so you can buy and sell bonds whenever you like. The bond will have a different price each day and can also fluctuate throughout the day, just like shares do.

The price of a bond will go down if interest rates go up and will go up if interest rates go down. The simplest way to have that make sense is to think about it this way. If you buy a bond from the Australian Government, it might pay 2 per cent interest for ten years. If the government then issues another ten-year bond that is paying 3 per cent interest, instead of the 2 per cent your existing bond pays, you'd rather sell the old one and buy the new one paying 3 per cent to get the better return. As a consequence, this increase in interest rates pushes down the price of old bonds because of the selling pressure. The reverse is also true, if the government came out with a bond only paying 1 per cent, people would rather buy the one you hold that pays 2 per cent, and so will pay you more to buy your bond from you.

The return on a bond will come partly from the income payments and partly from this up and down (movement in value) over time. Unlike cash and term deposits, bonds are not government guaranteed, so if you purchased a bond from a large Australian Stock Exchange (ASX)–listed company, for example, and that company collapsed, you would likely lose the money you had invested in that bond.

Bonds are a little more risky than cash and term deposits but are generally considered less risky than shares. Your superannuation fund likely has some of your superannuation invested in bonds. Bonds are often used to build a portfolio to provide a degree of stability, and they can often move up or down in value in the opposite direction to what the share market might do.

3. Shares

When you own shares, you are part owner of a business. That business might be small (e.g. you might own some or all of the local florist) or it might be large (e.g. you might own some shares in the Commonwealth Bank of Australia).

Whether big or small, you are a part owner of a business, and as such, you get to share in the ongoing prosperity (or failure) of that business. The smaller the business, the closer you (as a shareholder) may be to the day-to-day operations and decision making that goes into the running of that business. The reverse is true of large businesses. If you own $5000 worth of Commonwealth Bank shares, you have next to no influence in the day-to-day operations of the business. With large, stock market–listed businesses, you only hear about how the business is performing every six months when they give their update to the 'market' and everyone (owners of the business and the public) finds out at the same time.

When you own shares in a business, the return on your investment will generally come from two sources:

1. Dividends: These are your share of the profit that the business has generated and decided to distribute to shareholders. Often only part of the profits generated are distributed to shareholders as dividends; the business retains some profit to invest back into the business to grow the business. If management of the business is successful in this, you'd typically see increased profits and dividends in the years to come.

2. Share price movement: Hopefully, this is heading in an upward trajectory and reflects growing profits and increasing value of the business over time. However, as I'm sure you will have seen in the media, the value of your shares can and do move around day to day. The daily movements of share prices aren't a fair representation of the long-term value of most businesses as, from one day to the next, it's highly unlikely anything material will have changed with those businesses, but nonetheless, it's something you need to be aware of and deal with.

With technology advancements over the years, it's now possible to invest in shares with as little as a dollar or two. Investing directly into share markets is no longer out of reach for everyday Australians.

From July 1994 to June 2024, the annual return for the Australian stock market averaged out at 9.1 per cent. That's quite incredible when you think that $10 000 invested back on 1 July 1994 would have been worth $137 626 by 30 June 2024.

Investing in the stock market is not gambling, like some people might tell you. An investor is purchasing a part ownership of a business with a view that those in charge of running that business will be doing what they need to to ensure the ongoing prospects and success of that business. Over time, your ownership in that business will hopefully become worth more and you'll benefit from increased profit distribution in the form of dividends.

The shares that you purchase may be here in Australia or they may be in businesses in another country. Again, with advancements in technology, the barrier to you purchasing shares in an Australian business listed on the stock market here in Australia or any other business listed on major stock markets around the world has practically been eliminated. All you need is an account with any one of the numerous investing apps or online brokers that will let you purchase shares and you're ready to go.

When it comes to share investing, you can do this via a multitude of different means. Firstly, you can invest in individual business directly (i.e. you can, through your share broking account, go and buy Commonwealth Bank of Australia shares). Owning individual stocks or businesses isn't a great place to start when you first start buying shares as sometimes you may pick a poor performing company, watch your investment go backwards, then get scared off the share market before you've had time to really learn about it. To get a broad spread of businesses in different industries, doing different things, you're likely to need quite a lot of money to spread around the different businesses — and that's not feasible for most people just starting out on their journey with shares.

ETFs

Exchange traded funds (ETFs) or index funds have boomed in popularity over the last ten years or so. Through ETFs, your one investment is split across what could be several hundred different businesses. This allows you to very cheaply and very easily spread your money out across a range of different businesses in one go. The ETFs will be invested in line with a particular investing theme; for example, they may track an index such as the ASX200, which is a measure of the 200 biggest companies in Australia (this would be an index fund, explained shortly), or it could track the S&P500, which is a measure of the 500 biggest companies in America.

An index fund (or index ETF) is invested in the businesses that make up the particular index the investment is designed to track. The most common form of index fund (or index ETF) is invested in those businesses in the same proportion or ratio that they make up of the particular index they follow. The following table lists the top ten holdings for an ASX200 index investment at 23 February 2025. So for every $100 you invested into this investment, $10.22 would then be invested in CBA shares, $8.43 would be invested in BHP, $5.04 in CSL and so on.

While this table only lists the top 10 holdings, of your $100 investment $47.10 would be invested in these 10 businesses. Your remaining $52.90 would be invested across the other 190 businesses that make up the ASX200.

Stock code	Company name	Sector	Weight (per cent)
CBA	Commonwealth Bank of Australia	Financials	10.22
BHP	BHP Group Ltd	Materials	8.43
CSL	CSL Ltd	Health care	5.04
NAB	National Australia Bank Ltd	Financials	4.34
WBC	Westpac Banking Corporation Corp	Financials	4.29
WES	Wesfarmers Ltd	Consumer discretionary	3.48
ANZ	ANZ Group Holdings Ltd	Financials	3.45
MQG	Macquarie Group Ltd Def	Financials	3.26
GMG	Goodman Group Units	Real estate	2.66
TLS	Telstra Group Ltd	Communication	1.93

With index investing, you end up with more money invested in the bigger businesses and less money invested in the small businesses. This isn't necessarily good or bad, it's just how it is and something you need to understand as an investor in index funds.

Some ETFs track more niche parts of the stock market; for example, there is an investment that tracks the performance of the top battery manufacturers in the world. Then there are other ETFs that are described as 'active', and they follow the same investment approach that managed funds do, which I'll explain next. ETFs are purchased through your investing app or broking account just like you might purchase CBA shares.

MANAGED FUNDS

Managed funds were incredibly popular (they still are) before the boom in stock market–listed investment opportunities such as ETFs. Most of the time, although not always, a managed fund is described as 'active'. They differ from the ASX200 investment I described previously in that, instead of just having a small investment in each of the 200 biggest businesses on the Australian stock market, the managed fund manager will take an 'active' position by picking businesses they think are better than others. They will buy more of the ones they think are good, less of the ones they think are okay and none of the ones they think are bad. The managed fund may have investments in 20 or 30 different businesses, whereas an ETF might have investments in hundreds.

WHICH IS BETTER: ETFs OR MANAGED FUNDS?

The answer to this question depends on what you are looking for from the investment. There's lots of research that says, over the long run, very few active managed funds outperform low-cost index-style ETFs or investments. However, there are shorter periods of time where they do outperform each other. If you're just starting out, the low-cost index-style of investing is a fantastic place to start. As you build a substantial share portfolio, you may benefit from having smaller positions in some active funds that deliver different returns to the index investments at different points in time.

Managed funds are typically accessed by going direct to the particular investment manager. They may have some type of application form you need to complete before you transfer them money to make your investment. Depending on the type of investing app or broking account you use, you may have access to a range of managed funds directly through your account.

4. Property

Aussies love their property. From the great Australian dream of owning your own home to the often default position lots of Australian's take when they turn their attention to investing and buy an investment property.

Property investment may be in the form of a real asset such as a house or an apartment, or a shop, factory or some other commercial property. It could also be as shares in a real estate investment trust (more on this on page 89).

As with investments in the share market, your return on the property investment will come in two forms:

1. income or rental return

2. increase in value or capital growth.

When you buy a house and rent that property out to a tenant, the rent you receive from the tenant is the income component of your return. Depending on how you've funded the purchase of the property, you may need to use that rent plus some of your own cash to help pay off a mortgage. If you don't have a loan on the property, you'll be able to keep the rental income and use it to help fund your retirement. The other way you'll earn a return from the property is through the increase in its value that tends to occur over time — but not all properties go up in value over time.

Unlike the stock market, you can't invest in the 'property market' in the same way you can the stock market. With property, you buy one individual property on one street in one suburb in one part of Australia. Then, depending on what happens to that particular part of Australia, you will earn a return on the investment property you have purchased. That may be a fantastic positive return over an extended period of time, like those who have invested in and around Sydney have experienced, or the value of your property investment might have gone sideways for 15 years, like lots of investors in Darwin have experienced.

You can use debt to purchase both shares and property, but in my experience from speaking with thousands of people in my work as a financial adviser, people are generally more comfortable borrowing money to purchase an investment property than they are borrowing money to buy shares. Also, given the cost to purchase a property in Australia, most people generally need to borrow money if they are going to buy investment property, whereas you might be able to self-fund a few thousand dollars in shares.

It's the use of debt to fund one investment purchase (property) versus no debt to purchase another (shares) that delivers the different dollar value return investors earn when they look at shares versus property. Average returns from both asset classes are close enough to being the same. As I discussed earlier on page 67, the more money you borrow, the bigger the value of the asset you are able to purchase and, in turn, the likely better return you will earn over time (all other things being equal). But also don't forget what can happen when you borrow money and your investment goes down in value (see page 68).

REAL ESTATE INVESTMENT TRUSTS

Real estate investment trusts are stock market–listed businesses that own properties, among other things. Often they will own office buildings, warehouses or shopping centres. I'm not aware of any that own residential properties.

There are typically a variety of activities linked to a real estate investment trust, which could include:

- ownership of the types of properties I just mentioned

- development of those properties

- management of the tenants and general upkeep of the properties

- funds management operations.

The funds management operations are similar to the managed funds I discussed on page 87. They may manage a pool of money that, depending on the individual managed fund, might be invested into other stock market–listed real estate investment trusts, or the fund could be investing directly into the ownership of buildings.

Managed funds that invested directly into the ownership of buildings got into a whole lot of trouble during the global financial crisis (GFC) when they couldn't borrow money and investors wanted their money back. At the time, it caused a number of the managed funds that had invested into owning buildings directly to freeze redemptions.

Investors could only get their money back after the buildings the fund owned were sold, and some of those buildings sold for a lot less than the value people had invested into the funds, and as a result, investors got back less than they invested. This is one of the risks you need to accept when you decide to invest. Let's look a little more closely at the risks.

Risks with investing

All investing comes with a degree of risk.

The risks vary depending on the type of investing you do — there are different risks with investing in shares than there are investing in property, for example.

It's most important that you *manage* the risks as you can't really avoid them. Your ability to accept, manage and deal with the various risks that come with investing are, ultimately, what delivers the returns you desire. If you don't accept and manage the risks that come with investing, you won't earn the returns and you'll be stuck having to accept bank interest as your only return. That's not going to get you very far on your journey to retire life ready.

There are whole books dedicated to understanding investing and, in turn, the risks associated with it. I'm not going to go into that level of depth here, but I do want to ensure you have some understanding of what you may be getting into.

See the further resources section at the end of the book for some recommendations if you want to more detail on this (just finish this book first ☺).

There are two key investment risks I help clients manage in the financial advice work I do that are important for you to understand and implement in your own plans:

1. Avoid being a panicked seller.

2. Avoid being a forced seller.

1. Avoiding being a panicked seller

In order to manage the risk of being a panicked seller, you need to accept that your investments will go up and down over time on your journey to building your net nest egg balance and retiring life ready.

No-one panics that their investments have gone up too much; the panic starts with a downturn in whatever market you are investing in. Let's play out a hypothetical scenario: so the market has just gone down, and you're panicking and sell out thinking you'll reinvest when things bottom out or start to look better again. The problem is how will you ever know when the market has bottomed? Who will tell you? What's your sign for things to be better for you to reinvest?

If the markets continue to fall, you will pat yourself on the back for making the right call, but you probably won't invest again just now as it might fall some more. So you wait and you wait. Then, all of a sudden, things start to go up … but you know they will go back down again so you wait and you wait. What's the trigger for you to reinvest?

These are all questions with answers nobody knows, so it's important you aren't a panicked seller, and instead, are investing in a manner you are comfortable with so that you can ride out the inevitable ups and downs.

In my work as a financial adviser, we always ask clients a question (among others) along the lines of: 'How far are you willing to accept your portfolio may drop before things have gone too far for you?' Responses from clients vary from minus 5 per cent, minus 10 per cent, minus 15 per cent and minus 20 per cent.

Most of the time, although not always, the younger someone is, the more likely they are to pick the minus 20 per cent answer because they have time on their side for things to recover. Often an answer of minus 20 per cent comes with a comment along the lines of: 'I'm okay to go down if the whole market has gone down, but if my investments have gone down and the market has gone up, then there's something wrong.' I agree with this comment! We use this question (and others) to determine someone's attitude towards investing, and this helps us guide an appropriate investment mix.

Client story: Cashing out when the going gets tough

In all the years I've worked in financial advice, I've only ever had one client sell out twice, and it did a huge amount of damage to their retirement savings.

Let's call this client Wendy. Wendy earned an average income but put a little extra into superannuation each year so she had built up a balance of over $500 000. Wendy and her husband had a mortgage on their own home that they were not going to be able to pay off by the time they reached 65, and they were always going to need to access Wendy's super to clear the mortgage when retirement came.

If we go back to 2008/2009, the GFC hit and caused share markets (and, as a result, superannuation balances) to fall significantly. At this stage, Wendy was still 15 years off retiring. As markets began to fall, Wendy started panicking. She watched her super balance drop and she started calling me regularly. My advice to her every time she called was to leave her super balance alone; things

(continued)

would eventually turn around. She was 15+ years off from retiring, and had plenty of time to ride things out.

In March 2009, Wendy had had enough. She instructed me to move her whole superannuation balance to the cash investment option in her super account and said she would reinvest 'when things got better'. The day after she made the switch, markets dropped a little more. By 9 March 2009, stock markets around the world bottomed and started to recover. Wendy was convinced things would drop further so didn't reinvest her super. Almost a year later, I convinced her to reinvest half her super balance. In the years that followed, she reinvested the remaining balance but would always say to me 'super never recovered since the GFC'.

In reality, the share markets and super balances had recovered, and we eventually reached all-time record highs again. If Wendy had not sold out her super balance, she would also have had a super balance at the highest level it had ever been. Instead, her balance hovered around $300 000 after making some withdrawals once she turned 60 to pay for a few different things.

Fast-forward and we had the COVID market downturn. Wendy was a whole lot closer to retirement by now, but she went one better than she did during the GFC. This time Wendy picked the absolute bottom of markets during COVID to tell me she'd had enough and wanted to sell out. Fortunately, I convinced her to hold onto some of her investments so the damage wasn't as bad the second time around.

Wendy has now retired, cashed out all her superannuation and paid off their mortgage. She doesn't have any superannuation left. Had she not been a panicked seller, Wendy would have had several hundred thousand left in her superannuation fund after the withdrawal to clear the mortgage.

If you can't accept that your investments may go down from time to time, you shouldn't be investing. You can't expect to earn the good returns when times are good and not endure some of the poor returns when things aren't so great. You either need to accept bank interest as your return or spend some more time educating yourself on investment markets to ensure you reach retirement in a strong financial position that supports your ideal lifestyle.

DOLLAR COST AVERAGE

The way we like to tackle share market investing is via a strategy known as *dollar cost averaging*. Using this strategy, you invest an amount of money (often a fixed amount) at regular intervals into the stock market, no matter what the value of the stock market might be.

Using this strategy, you buy more units of your chosen investment when the price is lower and you buy fewer units of the investment when prices are higher. Take the following table, for example.

Investment amount	Unit price	Units purchased
$1000	$22	45
$1000	$23	43
$1000	$24	42
$1000	$18	56
$1000	$16	63
$1000	$15	67
$1000	$19	53
$1000	$22	45

Through regular $1000 investments, $8000 has been invested in this scenario. In the beginning, the value of the investment started going up (as an investor, you'd feel good about yourself here), then it fell quickly through the middle section (you wouldn't be feeling so good) before making its way back to $22 by instalment eight.

So the 'investment return' was actually zero. It started at $22 and finished at $22. For the up, down and up you had to endure, it finished where it started — not such a great investment.

Or was it?

Over the eight instalments, we invested $8000. Those instalments purchased 414 units. If each unit was worth $22 at the end that makes the total value of the investment $9108 (414 x $22). This means a return of $1108 was earned on the $8000 invested, which equates to a 13.85 per cent return — sounds like a good return to me.

What I've just described is the 'investors' return'. This is the return the individual investor earned, which is different to the 'investment return'. The investment returned zero — it ended at the same value it started. But because the investor kept investing through the ups and downs, the 'investors' return' was far better than the 'investment return'.

As crazy as this may sound, I often explain to people who are early in their journey to retire life ready that the best thing that can happen to them on their investing journey is that there is a big share market drop early on in the journey. This allows you to invest more and more money at lower and lower prices (as per the example I just showed you), and then, when things inevitably turn around, that's where you start to really magnify your wealth.

For those keen to turn the dial up on a dollar cost averaging strategy, you can take another step and invest more money when the market drops by a certain percentage. You might be investing $1000 at regular intervals, but if the market drops by 5 per cent, for example, you could add an extra $1000 following the drop before continuing on with your regular $1000 investments. This allows you to buy even more shares when things are down, so that you benefit even more on the way back up again.

Avoid being a forced seller

Avoiding being a forced seller means you aren't forced to sell growth assets for your spending needs. It comes down to your ability to access cash when you need it. During your working life, you work to earn an income, and you spend that living and doing the things you want to do. Hopefully you are putting aside some of what you earn for your future self so you can retire life ready.

However, things change when you stop working and you need income from your investments to support your lifestyle. Growth becomes less important than your ability to get your hands on cash from your investments to live off. This is where the type of assets you hold and the mix of those assets or investments becomes very important.

Ideally, you don't want to be set up in a way that you are forced to sell investments because you need the cash to live off. If you are a forced seller, inevitably, you'll have to sell at a time that isn't ideal (perhaps the value of your investments has just dropped for some reason), which, as my client Tony found out back on page 93, can cause a whole lot of damage to your retirement savings. Or even worse, without the right planning for your retirement income needs, you may have to sell an asset quickly, which then often means you just have to take whatever you are offered, perhaps less than the asset is actually worth.

What I typically find is that the assets you used to help you build your net nest egg assets up so that you can retire life ready are unlikely to be the same assets to take you through retirement. It's best you look at this as two distinct stages: the asset accumulation phase, which will require one mix of assets, and then the retirement income phase with a different set of assets for that stage. We often use an investment strategy called *three buckets* (discussed next) to help manage the retirement income phase.

Three-Bucket Investing Strategy

To help manage both the panicked seller and forced seller investment risks, I like the idea of using a strategy we call *three buckets*. This strategy becomes particularly useful once you've reached your net nest egg assets target, stopped working and begun to live off your retirement savings.

The strategy starts with your spending number per year that you worked out in Chapter 3. You use your spending number to help you allocate your net nest egg assets across the three buckets (see figure 5.5):

- Bucket 1: Your cash bucket has a balance equal to one year of your spending number.

- Bucket 2: Your fixed-interest bucket has a balance equal to three or four times your spending number.

- Bucket 3: Your growth bucket holds the balance of your net nest egg assets in shares and property.

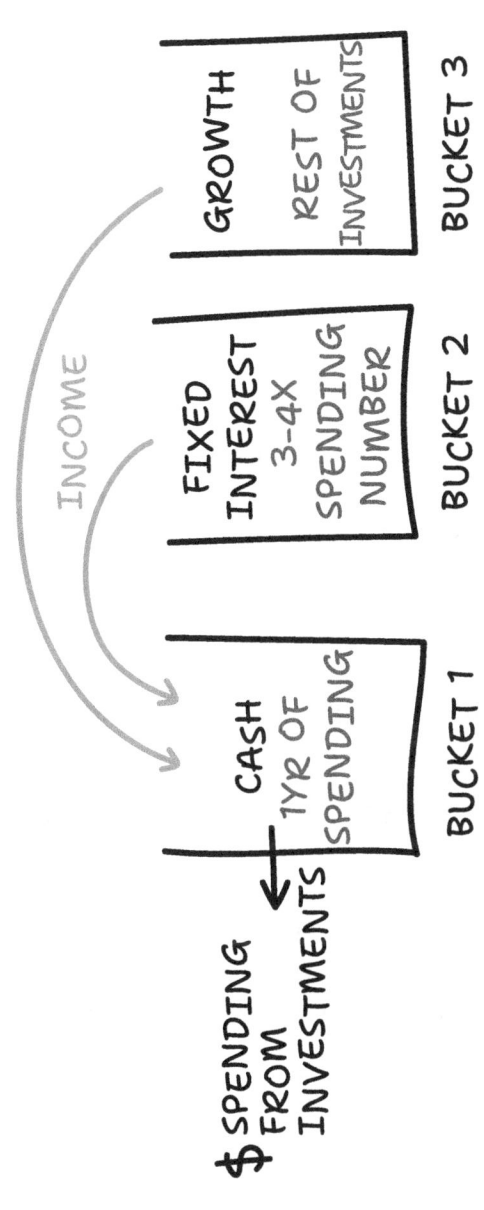

Figure 5.5: The Three–Bucket Strategy: Structuring your retirement income for access and longevity

You'll note the income arrows going across the top. You want to have any income you earn on your investments (buckets 2 and 3) paid out in cash and deposited into your cash account. Don't reinvest the dividends on your shares or the interest you earn on your term deposit — you need that cash to live off. It's then from the bucket 1 (the cash account) that you can set up a regular payment out into your everyday spending accounts and go about living that retirement you designed.

If you have assets in multiple structures, you would implement this same three-bucket approach within each of those structures. For example, if you had some money in a superannuation fund and also some money in a family trust, you'd start by working out how much of your spending number will be paid from your superannuation fund, then follow the three-bucket approach to allocate the money in your superannuation fund across the different buckets. Then, for your trust, determine how much of your spending number will be paid from the trust, then follow the three-bucket approach to allocate the money in your trust across the different buckets.

This strategy helps combat the panicked seller and the forced seller effectively.

- For the panicked seller, their third bucket that is made up of shares and property will go up and down in value with market movements. However, as they aren't relying on selling those assets to live off (instead, they are just collecting the income those assets generate), there's a degree of comfort. This comfort is further emphasised by having up to five years of their spending number in buckets one and two, which, given what they are invested in, aren't likely to go up or down in value much at all.

If bucket 3 has dropped and you need extra money out for some reason, just take it from bucket 1 or 2 and let bucket 3 recover over time.

■ For the forced seller, this strategy purposely sets up your assets so that you are, as much as possible, living off the income your assets generate, not the selling down of those assets. As I mentioned earlier, if something does come up that you need extra money for, you can take it from bucket 1 or 2, leaving bucket 3 to do its thing. If your investments don't quite generate enough income for you, you can slowly draw down on buckets 1 and 2, leaving bucket 3 to continue to grow in value. Further, if you don't sell down your assets and instead just live off the income they generate, you'll still own the assets to be able to collect the income they generate next year, and the year after that and the year after that. This is how you make your assets last forever.

What investment when?

The final piece I want to leave you with in this chapter is understanding that the different assets I've described will be more appropriate for you at different stages as you work on closing the gap to retire life ready. As mentioned on page 98, what you built to close the gap before your dream retirement is unlikely to be appropriate for you in your actual retirement years, and it's important that you revisit the mix of the investments you hold.

Cash and fixed-interest investments are likely to be lower risk (and lower returns) than shares or property. For that reason, if you are early on in your journey and have 10+ years until you're targeting retirement, having a whole lot of money in these two assets probably isn't a great idea. However, as you get nearer and nearer retirement, they will become more important for you as you look to build up buckets 1 and 2.

I like the idea of switching your focus to build up buckets 1 and 2 when you're about three years out from retirement. Ideally, you aren't selling down your shares and property investments to fund buckets 1 and 2; instead, you fill those buckets through your regular savings and investing *plus* the income that your shares and property generate.

Property as an investment option works well for a lot of people to help them build their assets up. Most people borrow money to buy property, and as a result, they get magnified gains or exposure to the increase in the value of the property — because you're investing more than just your own cash (you're investing borrowed money too), this gives you an advantage if the value of the property increases over time. That, together with the 'forced savings' nature of having to make loan repayments to the bank, means you can't easily skip adding an amount of money to your investment, even if that money is just going back to the bank to pay your loan. Property also takes a long time to buy and sell (it's also quite costly), so for that reason, people are less likely to panic sell a property than they are shares, meaning you may end up holding it for a longer period of time and, therefore, benefiting from the growth over a longer period of time.

Using a residential investment property to fund your retirement isn't quite the same good idea. You'll recall from Chapter 3, I introduced you to the rule of 20x and the 4 per cent rule. Both were means of converting your desired retirement spending number into a target for your net nest egg asset to fund retirement.

The rule of 20x assumes you spend 5 per cent of your retirement capital each year, while the rule of 4 per cent assumes you spend 4 per cent. Now, as every investor in residential property will tell you, after you've paid land tax, council rates, strata or body corporate, agents fees, repairs and maintenance, maybe income tax, you are not likely to net (meaning after all costs and expenses) a rental return of 5 per cent or 4 per cent from your residential investment property — it's quite likely to be closer to 2 per cent.

So, when you've done all your retirement planning on the assumption you'll spend 5 per cent of your retirement capital each year using the rule of 20x or 4 per cent of your retirement capital using the 4 per cent rule, only to generate 2 per cent spending money from your residential investment property, something has to give. You either end up spending more of your other assets to make up the shortfall, causing you to spend through those assets at a much faster rate than you initially anticipated, or you end up selling the residential investment property at some point during your retirement. The only way holding most of your retirement savings in residential investment properties works is if you have lots and lots of money invested in property, with the debts paid off. For property to work, you'll need a lot more money invested in property than either the rule of 20x or the 4 per cent rule to guide you.

Shares work for both the closing-the-gap stage and through the retirement stage of your journey. Property would hold a slight advantage during the closing-the-gap stage, purely because, as I mentioned, you're most likely investing a bigger (borrowed) amount that benefits you as that property grows in value. On the other hand, not many people borrow money for shares, so they are only getting the return on their own invested cash.

Shares have the advantage over property when it comes time to draw an income because, not only is there a lot less expense (read: next to none) associated with the holding of shares, so you don't have that expense eating into your income, the income return from the Australian share market tends to be around 4 per cent and comes with the tax advantage of franking credits.

Franking credits are a refund of tax that the company you've invested in has paid before they pay a dividend out to you. To put it simply, the company has paid tax on their profits, which they then distributed to their shareholders. Franking credits prevent the same dollar of profit being taxed twice — once in the hands of the company and once in your hands. If your income is low enough (or you hold those shares in a super fund, for example), those franking credits can be refunded back to you in cash, which boosts the cash income that the shares pay you.

The other major advantage that shares have over property is that you can sell a portion of your shares to access the cash if you need it for some reason. It's only a day or two from the time you sell the share to when the money is in your bank account. Obviously, with property, you can't sell part of the house if you need some cash, and the length of time between deciding to sell and having the cash in your bank account is likely to be three or four months at best.

It's quite common to see people sell down some or all of their investment property portfolio to move that money into more liquid (easily sellable) and higher-income paying assets (often shares and term deposits) when they get to retirement. If this is you, following the three-bucket approach I outlined on page 98 is a great idea.

Retire life ready steps

Write down what assets you hold in the four broad investing asset types from page 77:

Cash $_____

Bonds $_____

Shares $_____

Property $_____

It's likely that there is one type you are more comfortable investing in, either because you have always had assets invested that way or because it's a type of asset you know more about.

The type of asset I am most comfortable investing in is: _____

Is there another asset type that could help strengthen your retire life ready position or that you would like to start investing in? If so, what is it? _____

What steps could you take right now to explore this investing type for your future?

_____

_____

Next, we'll explore the tax implications of your finances from your everyday personal tax on your income to how you can structure your finances for more beneficial tax outcomes. Each comes with its own pros and cons, but with some careful thought, you can use it to build your net nest egg assets for your future retirement.

CHAPTER 6

Keeping more of your hard-earned by understanding tax

Let's follow up the conversation about investing with one about tax — everyone's favourite topic. I get so many questions from people trying to minimise their tax or complaining that they are paying too much tax, but there's a difference between not liking how much tax you pay and paying too much of it.

When you lodge your tax return each year, that's when, if you have paid too much tax, you get a refund, or if you haven't paid enough tax, you'll get a bill. You might not like the total amount of tax you've paid, but it's really just a reflection of the income you've earned. The more you earn, the more tax you pay, but most importantly, the more you get to keep too.

Tying this in with investing from Chapter 5, you should never be investing for the tax benefit that investments provide you in isolation. You should be investing in a way that will help you close the gap on your desired net nest egg number but also invest with the tax outcomes in mind. Ultimately, if you can own that same investment in a way that means you pay a bit less tax, you then get to keep more of the return, and it puts you that much closer to your net nest egg number.

Let me explain how personal taxes and your investing work, some of the most common structures you might use to better manage your tax situation, and how deductions work.

Personal taxes

As an individual, each year you are required to lodge a tax return if your income is above the tax-free threshold, and pay the appropriate amount of tax on the income you've earned. That's one tax return where all the income you earn from every source gets added together and taxed according to the marginal tax-rate system.

For a typical person this might include things like your:

- salary from work
- bonus from work
- interest on a bank account
- dividends on shares you own.

For someone with slightly more complicated financial affairs, it might also include things like:

- the vested value of stock in the company you work for
- capital gains on an investment you sold (more on this next).

We have a progressive tax system here in Australia. As your income increases over certain thresholds ($45 001 or $135 001, for example) the rate of tax you pay on every extra dollar increases.

Everyone gets the benefits of the lower tax brackets though. For example, if you earned $350 000 in the 2024–25 financial year, the first $18 200 you earn is tax free. The vast majority of working Australians will sit in the band covering $45 001 to $135 000 and pay 30 cents' tax on every extra dollar of income they earn in that band, until their income goes over $135 001.

It's your income, after deductions, that is taxed at the marginal tax rates. The tax rates for Australian residents for the 2024–25 year are as follows.

Taxable income	Tax on this income	Marginal tax rate
$0–$18 200	Nil	0%
$18 201–$45 000	16c for each $1 over $18 200	16%
$45 001–$135 000	$4288 plus 30c for each $1 over $45 000	30%
$135 001–$190 000	$31 288 plus 37c for each $1 over $135 000	37%
$190 001 and over	$51 638 plus 45c for each $1 over $190 000	45%

Source: © Commonwealth of Australia.

In addition to the tax rates mentioned here, you'll also pay a Medicare levy on your taxable income if your income is over $93 000 for a single person or $186 000 for a family and you don't have private health insurance. The surcharge will be between 1 per cent and 1.5 per cent, depend on some factors, such as your taxable income.

As your income grows, and importantly, as you build up investments and start to earn income outside of what you earn from work, you need to understand how that will impact the tax you pay. If there's a way of paying less tax or holding that same investment in a different structure that doesn't pay ordinary personal tax rates, there's likely to be some advantage for you.

If you're an employee earning a wage, there is very little you can do about the structuring of your income to help better manage your tax situation. The ATO has designed it this way on purpose. They know you need to work to pay bills and live, and they don't need to incentivise you to do it.

Your employer will deduct the necessary amount of tax via their payroll system and pay it to the ATO for you. You might have some deductions you can claim (discussed in the next section), but outside of that, there's not a whole lot you can do about it. If this is you, I'd advise you to not make your tax situation any worse by earning more investment income in your personal name, which you'll pay further marginal tax on, and you can do this by using some of the investing structures I'll discuss later in this chapter.

On the other hand, business owners have a whole lot more flexibility. Again, this is on purpose. The ATO is incentivising people to have a go, take a risk and run a business. Small businesses are the biggest employers of people in Australia, and without the ATO incentivising those willing to give it a go and create businesses that, in turn, employ many others, the jobs just wouldn't exist. Business owners have the ability to pay themselves a wage (and pay ordinary taxes on that wage), but they can also use tax structures to distribute business profits out to entities that may pay lower rates of tax than individuals do (I'll explore some of this later in the chapter). If this is you, it's important you work closely with a good accountant, not one that just does your tax return, but one that actually provides you some proactive advice.

Capital gains tax

A capital gain occurs when you sell an asset (maybe shares or a property) for more than what you purchased it for. Under the Australian tax system, you then need to pay some tax on that gain.

We don't have a rollover system that allows you to roll over your gain into your next investment without paying tax on it, like the ones that exist in other countries (except for small business operators — if that's you, speak to your accountant). The capital gain is taxed in your own name just the same way as your salary is, and, for an individual, doesn't have its own special rate of tax. You'll pay the same amount of tax on a $100 000 assessable capital gain as you would a $100 000 salary from work. However, if you have owned the asset you sold for more than 12 months, only half of the gain is added to your income total and then taxed according to the marginal tax schedule.

Deductions

Tax deductions aren't quite what the name suggests. Sure, your tax reduces, but these are actually *income* deductions. Your income reduces as a result of the expense paid (deduction), and when you earn less income you pay less tax. Deductions do not reduce your tax bill dollar for dollar.

Let me explain with an example.

Imagine Julie earns $120000 + superannuation from her job as an interior designer for a big ASX-listed property group. On Julie's $120000 income, she would pay $29188 in tax and the Medicare levy.

If Julie had a tax deduction she could claim for $10000, her taxable income (income minus deductions) becomes $110000, and as a result she would pay $25988 in tax and the Medicare levy. So, the $10000 tax deduction isn't worth $10000 in tax saving to her, it's only worth $3200. It's better than nothing, but it's also not the $10000 that some might think the tax deduction is worth.

The most common deductions people might claim in their tax return are:

- work-related expenses (uniforms, tools, phones, laptops etc.)

- work-related motor vehicle expenses

- superannuation contributions (more on this in Chapter 7)

- donations to charity

- negative gearing (more on this on page 113).

Tax deductions come off the last dollar you earn. In Julie's example, her salary puts her in the 30 per cent marginal tax-rate bracket, but she still gets the benefit of the tax-free threshold, plus the first tax bracket up to $45000 where she pays 16 per cent tax. The deduction comes off her income, which, at $120000, puts her in the 30 per cent bracket. If Julie earned more, and her income put her in the 37 per cent or 45 per cent tax brackets, the tax deduction would be worth more as it would come off the portion of her income that is taxed in that highest bracket. As she pays more tax in those higher brackets, the reduction in her income and, therefore, reduction in tax is worth more to her.

The reverse is also true. If Julie's income was between $18 200 and $45 000, her marginal tax rate would only be 16 per cent and, as a result, the tax deduction would be worth less to her.

Negative gearing

Negative gearing is the name given to the situation where you borrow money to buy an investment, then the costs of borrowing that money and the costs of holding the investment outweigh the income you earn from that investment. Where the costs outweigh the income you earn, you are able to claim the difference as a tax deduction against any other income you earn, and as a result, have a portion of that difference refunded as part of your tax return.

Let's continue with Julie's example. Say, for example, Julie borrowed $600 000 to purchase an investment property. On that $600 000 of borrowings, Julie would pay interest of around 7 per cent or $42 000. Julie would also have some other outgoing expenses on that property, like land tax, council rates etc., and she would also earn rental income. If the difference between the income earned, interest paid and other outgoings paid meant that Julie was out of pocket $10 000, then Julie would be able to claim that difference in her tax return using the same principles we used in the first example. The cost of being out of pocket $10 0000 would result in a tax refund of $3200, but Julie would still be out of pocket $6800.

As you can see from Julie's example, the negative gearing on the investment property is helping Julie pay less tax. However, even though Julie gets a tax refund of $3200, she is still out of pocket $6800. Holding the investment has cost her more than the income she has earned on that investment. Now, if the investment Julie purchased isn't growing in value by at least $6800 per year (or, even worse, is going down in value), Julie is going backwards financially. Buying that investment would have then been a poor decision, and if there is no catalyst for the value of the investment to turn around and start growing at the required rate, the longer Julie held that investment, the worse financial position she would be in.

Client story: Restructuring your retirement nest egg

Australian's love their property and they love their negative gearing even more. I recently did some work for a couple who, when they first came to see me, didn't think they would ever be able to retire. This couple were self-employed and, at the age of 60, only had $450 000 in superannuation between them. Like many self-employed people, they hadn't prioritised contributing to superannuation, but had purchased three investment properties. All three were negatively geared, meaning they were costing more to hold than the rent they were receiving — they had to top-up the shortfall with their income from work.

It was impossible for them to hold the three investment properties and retire. They would have needed to use their $450 000 in superannuation to support their living needs as well as cover the shortfall on their investment properties. At best, their super would last them four years.

I was able to show them that they had a lot of money tied up in the properties and that, if they kept them, they would have to keep working forever, but if they *sold* them, they could boost their combined superannuation balances to around $1.6 million and comfortably retire. Tax-deductible superannuation contributions would help with capital gains tax and staggering the sales across different financial years would reduce the tax burden even more so they could comfortably retire.

Tax offsets

Where tax deductions (see page 111) reduce your taxable income, and as a consequence, result in you paying less tax, tax offsets reduce your tax payable dollar for dollar.

Some common tax offsets are for things like:

- super spouse contributions

- private health insurance

- seniors and pensions

- medical expenses.

The spouse super contribution tax offset, for example, allows one member of a couple to contribute money to their spouse's superannuation fund. With the contributor receiving a tax offset of up to $540. See Chapter 7 for more detail.

Where possible, it makes sense to make use of any tax offsets you may have available to you.

Tax structures

As I explained on page 108, individuals pay tax at marginal tax rates. All their income from all the sources they earn gets added together and taxed according to the marginal tax rates.

On the other hand, there are various entities you may hold investments in where those entities themselves pay tax at certain rates or give you the flexibility to distribute income to other people or entities for them to pay tax on the income.

Some of those entities are:

- superannuation
- companies
- trusts
- investment or insurance bonds.

Superannuation

I won't cover superannuation in any detail here as I'll cover it at length in Chapter 7, but just know superannuation is the lowest tax-rate structure we have available to us in Australia. So low, in fact, that it's possible to hold investments in superannuation and not pay any tax at all — *zero* — on any income or gains your investments inside super make for you.

Other than the tax free threshold, there is no other structure where you don't have to pay any tax on income earned.

Companies

Companies are separate legal entities that have their own tax file number and are required to lodge their own tax returns. Lots of people, when they own and operate their own business, do so through a company structure. Companies where 80 per cent or less of their assessable income is 'passive' (i.e. you are actually running a business, not just earning investment income), pay tax at the rate of 25 per cent.

Companies where more than 80 per cent of their assessable income is passive, pay tax at the rate of 30 per cent. For someone earning over $135 000, where their tax rate goes to 37 per cent and beyond, they could be better off holding investments in a company structure rather than their own name. Some of the wealthiest families have a large part of their wealth tied up in private companies because the earnings are only taxed at 30 per cent, rather than up to 45 per cent plus the Medicare levy.

In addition, a company doesn't have to pay the income or returns it earns out to anyone (it can if it wants to, but it doesn't have to), so the earnings can be retained inside the company to continue to grow the investments.

Unlike an individual who is only assessed as having to pay tax on half of a capital gain if the asset being sold has been held for more than 12 months, a company, where more than 80 per cent of its income is passive, will pay a flat rate of 30 per cent tax on capital gains. It does not get the 50 per cent reduction that an individual gets.

Companies can also have a franking account. Like we discussed on page 104, when a company pays tax, it builds up a franking account balance equivalent to the tax the company has paid. Later, when the company releases some of its money back to the shareholders in the form of a dividend (refer to shares in Chapter 5), those franking credits (or allowance for tax already paid) is also paid out to the shareholder. Depending on that shareholder's tax position at the time, they may qualify to have those franking credits refunded in cash, otherwise, they will be used to offset or reduce any tax payable on the dividend received.

Trusts

Trusts come in many different forms; for example, superannuation is a kind of trust. I'll explain the most common type here, which is a family trust.

A trust is a relationship between the trustee (the person controlling the trust and making decisions for the trust) and the beneficiaries of the trust (the people who can benefit from the money in the trust).

Like a company, a trust needs to lodge a tax return each year. Unlike a company, a trust does not itself pay tax unless it doesn't distribute its earnings to one or more of the trust beneficiaries. If it doesn't distribute its income, then the trust is taxed at the top marginal tax rate on all its income earned during that financial year.

Think of a trust like a pass-through entity. The investments of the trust are invested in whatever they are invested in, but by the end of the financial year, the earnings on those investments need to be paid out to one or more beneficiaries for the beneficiary to pay tax on. Given it's the beneficiary who pays tax on the earnings of the trust, if the trust distributes to an individual, that trust income will be added to the individual's other income and taxed according to the normal marginal tax-rate scales. If the trust distributes its income to a company, like the one just described, then the company will pay 30 per cent tax on the income it receives.

As for capital gains, it depends where they are paid. If a capital gain is paid to an individual, that individual can use the 50 per cent reduction in capital gain if the asset has been owned by the trust for more than 12 months, just the same as though the individual owned the investment themselves.

On the other hand, if the trust distributes the capital gain to a company, the company doesn't quality for the 50 per cent capital gain discount and will pay the flat 30 per cent tax.

As you can see, with this capital gains issue, a trust provides quite a degree of flexibility when managing your tax affairs.

Investment bonds

Investment bonds have been around for years. They fell out of favour for a number of years because of their high fees and poor returns on investment options, but with changes to how much you can contribute to superannuation, and the introduction of caps on superannuation balances, a lot of investment has gone into investment bonds in recent years making them far cheaper than they were and offering far better investment options. They now resemble the fee structure and investment menu available from most of the major superannuation funds.

An investment bond is an account, somewhat like a superannuation fund, that you can add money to and have that money invested in an investment option of your choice. The money you contribute to the bond is not tax deductible and is made with your post-tax income. The bond is internally taxed (similar to a superannuation fund) so that the income earned by the investments within the bond isn't added to your personal tax return, instead the bond pays tax on its earnings for you. An investment bond pays tax at the company tax rate of 30 per cent. If your income is over $135 000, or will get there with investment earnings in time, there could be a tax advantage in you investing via investment bonds rather than in your own name.

There are no limits to how much you can deposit into an investment bond. There is also no limit on the balance you can have in your investment bond. There are limitations (time or otherwise) on withdrawing money out of your investment bond, and there are a couple of key things to understand to help you make the most out of using your investment bond:

- The ten-year rule: This rule says that any money you withdraw from your bond ten years after you commenced the bond doesn't incur any extra tax on your investment gains (remember the bond has already paid 30 per cent tax on earnings). For withdrawals made in year nine, you only have to pay tax on one-third of the gains withdrawn; year eight, you pay tax on two-thirds of the gains withdrawn; and anything prior to year eight, you pay tax on all of the gain. But those withdrawn gains come with a 30 per cent tax offset (refer back to page 115 for an explanation of offsets).

- The 125 per cent rule: This rule says that if you contribute 125 per cent in one year more than what you contributed to your bond in the previous year, you will reset the ten-year clock (as per the ten-year rule). So you need to be really careful you don't trip up on this point. Your investment bond provider can help you track the 125 per cent.

Investment bonds can work really well for people earning over $135 000 who want to do some investing and would like to be able to access their money earlier than aged 60 (when they can access their superannuation). They also work really well for parents or grandparents wanting to set up some type of investment account for their children or grandchildren, as those under the age of 18 can only earn $416 in investment income before they have to pay the top marginal tax rate.

Retire life ready steps

As you can see, there is a lot to consider when it comes to effectively managing your taxes. For those working as an employee, there isn't a whole lot you can do to reduce the tax you pay (other than earning less), so shift your focus to not making your tax situation any worse than it might already be and try to keep investment income out of your individual tax return. Consider using some of the structures outlined in this chapter, so tax can be paid in some other entity, rather than in your personal name.

If you do own and operate your own business, you've got a lot more flexibility and you may end up with a set-up that looks something like this: Your business owned inside of a family trust that pays wages to you, super contributions to your super fund and dividends via the family trust to a range of beneficiaries (see figure 6.1, overleaf).

Remember, the more of your investment returns you get to hold onto, the faster you'll close the gap on your net nest egg number and be able to retire life ready.

What is your marginal tax rate ＿＿＿＿＿＿＿＿ and how much extra income can you earn in your own name before you go up to the next marginal tax rate? ＿＿＿＿＿＿＿

What deductions have you been claiming in your tax return?

＿＿＿＿＿＿＿＿＿＿＿＿＿＿＿＿＿＿＿＿＿＿＿＿＿＿＿

＿＿＿＿＿＿＿＿＿＿＿＿＿＿＿＿＿＿＿＿＿＿＿＿＿＿＿

＿＿＿＿＿＿＿＿＿＿＿＿＿＿＿＿＿＿＿＿＿＿＿＿＿＿＿

Is there anything extra you could be claiming in your tax return?

＿＿＿＿＿＿＿＿＿＿＿＿＿＿＿＿＿＿＿＿＿＿＿＿＿＿＿

＿＿＿＿＿＿＿＿＿＿＿＿＿＿＿＿＿＿＿＿＿＿＿＿＿＿＿

Which of the structures discussed in this chapter are you going to research further to see if there is benefit for you?

_____

_____

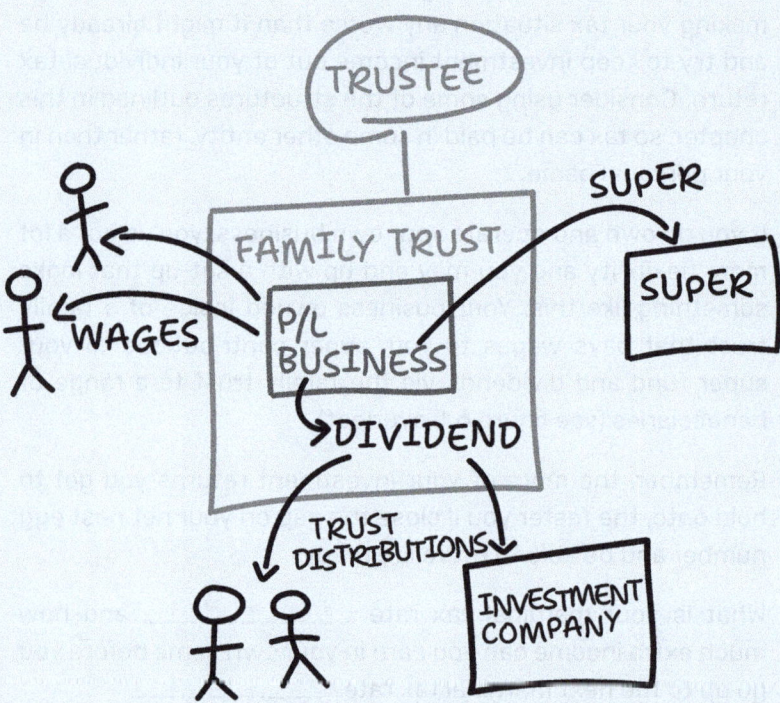

Figure 6.1: Family trust structures: How income flows through a business for tax-effective wealth building

CHAPTER 7

Superannuation is the backbone of your retirement

Superannuation is my favourite topic when it comes to you planning to retire life ready. Whether your plans are to be retired by age 40 or you're happy still going at age 65, superannuation *needs* to be part of your planning.

The Australian superannuation system is massive. As of May 2024, the total value of superannuation in Australia was over $3.5 trillion. This makes Australia the fourth-largest holder of pension-fund assets in the world. Government-mandated, employer-paid superannuation contributions, together with reasonable returns over time, mean the system keeps growing and growing.

For the average Australian, by the time they retire, their superannuation balance will be the second-biggest asset that they own after their home. However, for my most comfortable clients in retirement, the value of their superannuation and other investment assets outweigh the value of their own home at a ratio of at least 2:1. Meaning for every $1 of value they have in their own home, they have $2 in superannuation and other investments.

Given that superannuation will make up the backbone of your retirement, and you will have so much of your wealth in the super system by the time you do retire, it's important that you understand superannuation and how to make the most of it.

Even if you plan on retiring early (under the age of 60), superannuation should still be a big part of your retirement plans. If you are planning on retiring young, yes, it doesn't make sense to have all of your investment assets tied up in superannuation because you won't be able to access them until you are at least 60. However, it's highly likely you will eventually be 60 and enjoying your retirement for many years thereafter, so you'll need to have some money outside of superannuation to fund the earlier part of your retirement before you are old enough to access your super. But, you do want to have the bulk of your retirement assets in superannuation to benefit from the long-term tax concessions the system affords you.

If you're an employee, your employer has to contribute 12 per cent of your salary to superannuation for you. This rate of contribution has been on the rise for a few years before stopping at the current level of 12 per cent. Employers have been required to make contributions for their employees, albeit at much lower amounts, since 1 July 1992, which is 30-plus years ago, so it's not uncommon to see very healthy super balances at retirement.

If you are self-employed, there is no such mandating that you have to make superannuation contributions, the government leaves it up to you to decide if you want to contribute or not, and in my opinion, you'd be mad if you aren't.

A little pet peeve of mine is self-employed people who say, 'I don't have much super because I've been self-employed most of my life'. It's not because of your self-employment that you don't have much superannuation, it's because you haven't prioritised putting money into superannuation when you've been managing the cash flow of your business. Your cash has gone to current-day consumption in one form or another, rather than allocating some to longer-term retirement savings. If you're self-employed or a small business owner and you don't contribute anything to super, please change that and change it fast.

A tax structure, not an investment

The first thing I want you to understand about superannuation is that it's a tax structure, not an investment. This part is incredibly important so I'll say it a different way. Superannuation is a tax structure through which you can hold just about any investment you like, but there's an important difference.

Superannuation law, together with tax law, dictates when you can access your money, the tax you pay when you do access it and the tax paid on the earnings. You, the superannuation fund member, get to choose what your superannuation is invested in.

The superannuation tax structure is so generous that it is the lowest tax environment we have available to us here in Australia. The tax rates get so low, that you can pay zero tax on any income or capital gains you earn (regardless of the size of the income or gain) as well as pay zero tax on the money you take out of the system to spend and live off (regardless of how much you take out). Your only limitation on withdrawing money from the superannuation system, once you are over 60 and retired, is how much you have in your superannuation fund—take it all if you wanted (although probably not a great idea).

Superannuation explained

I've drawn this diagram hundreds, if not thousands, of times over the years I've been working in financial advice, and I still think it's both the easiest way for me to explain superannuation and the easiest way for you to understand it. What I'm about to explain is an accumulation-style account because that's what the vast majority of people have (see figure 7.1). You may be one of the few people that have a defined benefit; I'll touch on those on page 147.

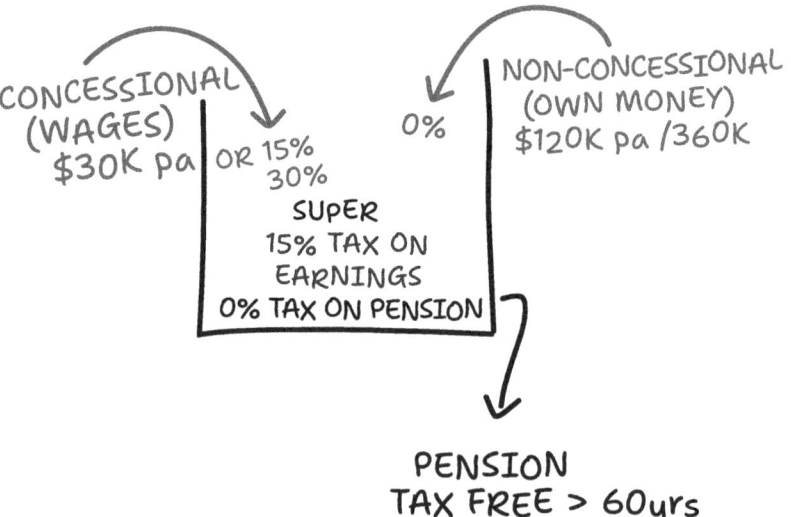

Figure 7.1: The superannuation bucket: How concessional and non-concessional contributions flow in

Think of superannuation like a bucket: money gets into your bucket one of two ways:

1. On the left side of the diagram, as part of your wages through the contributions your employer makes for you: The annual limit you can contribute is $30 000 per annum, including what your employer contributes. You can top-up the difference between what your employer makes for you and this $30 000 cap either through salary sacrifice or a deposit from your own cash holdings, and then provide your super fund with a form called a notice of intent-to-claim form. These contributions are called concessional contributions and are taxed when deposited into your superannuation fund at 15 per cent if your income is under $250 000 or 30 per cent if it is over. Any of your own money you contribute (and lodge the notice of intent-to-claim form for), you can claim as a tax deduction in your tax return. If you're self-employed, you can make these contributions for yourself.

2. On the right side of the diagram, after-tax deposits: This works by depositing your own after-tax money (savings you might have in a bank account, for example), transferring stock market–listed shares or commercial property. If transferring the latter two, please watch out for capital gains tax on the transfer. There's an annual limit of $120 000 per year, or you can group together the current year plus the next two financial years and put in up to $360 000 in one go (your ability to contribute like this is called 'bring forward'). These contributions are called non-concessional contributions and they aren't taxed when you deposit the money into your superannuation fund as you've already paid tax on this money yourself. You also can't claim a tax deduction for these contributions.

You can make concessional contributions regardless of your superannuation balance and provided you are under the age of 67. Between 67 and 75, you need to meet something called the work test, which says you've done 40 hours' worth of paid work over a 30-day period. Once you've met the work test, you can make concessional contributions for the financial year. You need to meet this test in every financial year you intend to make the concessional contribution if you're over the age of 67. After age 75, you can no longer make these contributions unless you are in paid employment and your employer has to make these contributions for you.

For non-concessional contributions, you can make them regardless of whether you are working up until the age of 75 — you don't need to meet the work test like you do for concessional contributions. However, as your total superannuation balance (being the sum of all interests you have in super, both accumulation and pension; see the next section for more on this) starts to approach $2 million, your ability to make these non-concessional contributions starts to reduce. If your total super balance was:

- under $1.76 million at the end of the previous financial year, you can contribute up to $360 000

- over $1.76 million but below $1.88 million at the end of the previous financial year, you can contribute up to $240 000

- over $1.88 million but below $2 million at the end of the previous financial year, you can contribute up to $120 000

- $2 million or over at the end of the previous financial year, you can't make any non-concessional contributions.

If you've used up your three-year non-concessional limit in one go, you need to wait for the next couple of financial years to pass and then you can contribute again, provided you are still under 75 by that time.

Tax on superannuation

While your money is in the bucket and you're building the balance up, your account will be in what's called the *accumulation phase.* Your superannuation fund in the accumulation phase will pay tax of 15 per cent on its earnings. Capital gains on assets held in a superannuation fund, for more than 12 months, qualify for a one-third discount on this tax rate, which means capital gains are only taxed at 10 per cent in superannuation for assets held longer than 12 months before disposal and 15 per cent for assets held for less than 12 months.

Think back to the tax rates I explained in Chapter 6, which individuals or companies pay on their earnings and capital gains. It's a big difference, isn't it? A top marginal tax-rate payer pays up to 47 per cent tax on their income and investment earnings in their own name, but only up to 15 per cent in their superannuation fund. Even for lower income earners, if you pay any tax at all on investment earnings in your own name, you would have paid less tax on that same investment earning if it was held inside of a superannuation fund. Think about that for a moment.

Your ability to contribute pre-tax money to superannuation and the incredibly low tax rates on earnings make it so attractive. You don't pay any tax at all on superannuation in the pension phase. So things are great in the accumulation phase, but even better once you can commence a pension.

Accessing your superannuation

The purpose of superannuation is to provide retirement benefits to members, or to their dependants if the member dies before retirement. It's not intended as a bucket you access in your younger years if you get into financial trouble. While it is possible to access your superannuation in very limited circumstances, it really isn't ideal if you're under the age of 60, and you'll be taxed heavily if you do so. Please try and have other emergency money elsewhere, and don't look to your superannuation fund to fill that gap. In order to access your superannuation, you first need to be old enough (this is known as preservation age), which is currently 60.

Transition to retirement

Once you turn 60, you can access your superannuation in the form of a transition to retirement income stream (TRIS) if you are still working. Under a TRIS, you can access between 4 per cent and 10 per cent of your account balance each financial year. You access that money in the form of a pension and it will be paid to you tax free. Your TRIS will still pay the same taxes (internally on investment earnings) as an accumulation account, as described on page 126.

Post–1 July 2017, a TRIS became far less attractive than it was prior to 1 July 2017. Since the earnings tax on a TRIS remains the same as an accumulation account, there is next to no benefit in commencing a TRIS unless you actually need the money. Prior to 1 July 2017, there was a tax advantage in commencing a TRIS, which doesn't exist anymore. Now there are really only three reasons you'd commence a TRIS:

1. You're winding down your employment and need a boost in your income (i.e. you're actually slowly transitioning to retirement, aren't earning enough from work to live your lifestyle, so access some of your super as a top-up).

2. You can't afford to maximise your concessional contributions up to the cap of $30 000 per annum while you are still working, so in order to ensure you can still live comfortably and maximise your superannuation contributions, you take a top-up from your super in the form of a TRIS. The low rate of tax on your super contribution and the tax-free pension you take out from your TRIS provides you with an overall tax advantage.

3. You are getting an early start on an estate planning strategy to increase the tax-free component of your superannuation, so you commence a TRIS to access up to 10 per cent of your superannuation balance tax free but then re-contribute that same amount back into superannuation as a non-concessional contribution, which boosts the tax-free component of your superannuation fund (more on this on page 198).

Case Study: How a TRIS can benefit you

Jack is 61 and starting to think seriously about his retirement planning. Jack works fulltime earning $65 000 per annum and has $320 000 in his superannuation fund. Jack hasn't ever contributed anything more to superannuation than what his employer has paid for him. Jack's friend mentioned something about a TRIS, and this has got Jack looking into the benefits.

(continued)

On Jack's $65000 income, his employer pays 12 per cent superannuation contributions ($7800). If we ignore any carry forward concessional contributions Jack might have available, just based on the current concessional contribution cap of $30000, Jack could salary sacrifice $22200 to take him up to his concessional cap.

	No salary sacrifice	Salary sacrifice to $30000 cap
Salary	$65000	$65000
Salary sacrifice	$0	$22200
Tax on income	$11563	$4357
Take-home pay	$53437	$38443
Employer super (12%)	$7800	$7800
Salary sacrifice	$0	$22200
Total super contribution	$7800	$30000
Less tax on super contribution	$1170	$4500
Net super contribution	$6630	$25500

By doing the salary sacrifice, Jack's take-home pay drops by $14994 (refer to the take-home pay row $53437 and $38443). Jack could commence a TRIS for the shortfall of $14994 from his $320000 superannuation balance so that his take-home pay remains the same. He will not pay any tax on this pension payment from his super fund. Remember, with a TRIS, you need to take out between 4 per cent and 10 per cent of your balance in pension payments each financial year.

As a result of the salary sacrifice, and after allowing for tax on super contributions, Jack is contributing an extra $19146.25 pa ($25500 - $6353.75) to his superannuation than he would have by just relying on his employer's contribution on his behalf. Then, if we subtract the $14994 in tax-free pension payments Jack takes back out of his superannuation, the net benefit of the TRIS strategy is $4152.25 each year. Certainly well worth Jack setting up.

Retirement-phase pensions

If you've stopped working, or change employers over the age of 60, you will then have full access to your accumulated superannuation benefits (not limited to the 10 per cent maximum like a TRIS). Once you meet one of these conditions, you can access your benefits either via lump sum withdrawal or an account-based pension. As with a TRIS, you can access this money tax-free.

If you've commenced an account-based pension, then the earnings tax on your superannuation fund goes to *zero* — you read that right, *zero*. No tax on earnings or capital gains, completely tax-free earnings and completely tax-free payments to you. There is no other structure in Australia that is so generous.

In order to maintain the tax-free status of your account-based pension, there is a minimum amount of money you need to take out of your account each year. As you get older, that minimum increases, eventually the minimum requirement will see the balance of your account-based pension start to drop — this is normal. This is the government's way of encouraging you to spend the money and not leave a big pile of it sitting inside your superannuation for future generations. While the money needs to be paid out of your pension fund, and the balance of your pension account may go down over time, that money doesn't disappear. If you don't spend it, it will just build up in your bank account. It is very common for my 80+-year-old clients to end up in a situation where they are building up cash savings or investments outside of superannuation as their lifestyle has slowed and they aren't spending the minimum amount they are forced to take in pension payments.

The minimum pension payments are a percentage of your pension account balance at the beginning of each financial year, and are based on your age at the beginning of the financial year, as per the following table (the same minimum requirement applies to a TRIS too).

Age on 1 July or (if commenced in the financial year) the commencement date	Minimum per cent of your account balance you must withdraw each year
Under 65	4 per cent
65 to 74	5 per cent
75 to 79	6 per cent
80 to 84	7 per cent
85 to 89	9 per cent
90 to 94	11 per cent
95+	14 per cent

Source: © Commonwealth of Australia.

During times of share market downturn, like during the GFC and COVID, the government reduced the minimums by half so as to limit the amount of money people have to take out of their pension funds when their balances are down. By doing this, the government is trying to stop people from being forced sellers at poor times in the markets, but if those same people had followed the three-bucket approach to managing their retirement savings, it wouldn't be quite the same problem. They need to read this book!

In recent years, the Australian Government has implemented restrictions on how much money you can have in an account-based pension. That currently stands at $2 million and is increased every few years in line with inflation, so if you are reading this book, check the current numbers. So the first $2 million you have in superannuation can be invested and accessed tax free. You can still access anything in excess of $2 million tax free, however, the money remains in the accumulation phase where the earnings are still taxed at 15 per cent on earnings and 10 per cent on long-term capital gains.

Account-based pensions and TRISs are incredibly flexible, in that you have tax free access to up to 10 per cent of your account balance each year in a TRIS, or full access to the total balance of your account in an account-based pension. They offer a choice of investment, so you are free to choose how your balance is invested in line with your own preferences.

However, the downside of both the account-based pension and the TRIS is that there is no guarantee of how long your account balance will last. How long your account balance lasts (before you run out of money) is a function of how much you start with, how much you spend each year and what your investment returns are. The more you spend or the lower the returns on your investments, the faster you'll spend through the balance.

If you're hitting your net nest egg assets number that you worked out in Chapter 3, and then investing in line with the three-bucket approach outlined in Chapter 5, the combination of the two will go a long way to ensuring the longevity of your account-based pension.

Downsizing

A major opportunity to boost your superannuation balance as you head towards retirement was introduced back in 2018 — it's called downsizing. The downsizing rule allows you to top-up your superannuation by up to $300 000 (tax free) from the proceeds of selling your house.

This type of contribution is called a downsizing contribution, but it actually has nothing to do with you needing to downsize in the sense you would typically use the word. The size or value of the house you buy or sell has nothing to do with it. Buy a bigger house if you like, you only need to satisfy the following three requirements to use the downsize contribution rules:

1. You must be over the age of 55 at the time you make the contribution.

2. You or your spouse must have owned the property for more than ten years.

3. The sale is at least partially exempt from capital gains tax as a result of you or your spouse living in the property as a primary residence.

Point 2 means it doesn't matter who owns the property being sold: You could own the property being sold, your partner or spouse could own it, or you could own it jointly. When the property is sold, you can both use proceeds from the sale of the house to make contributions to your respective superannuation funds.

Point 3 can cause some confusion. You don't have to be currently living in the property, you just have to have lived in it at some point during your ownership of the property so that at least part of the sale proceeds are exempt from tax under the main residence tax exemption.

You have 90 days from settlement of the sale of your property to make the contribution to your superannuation fund. You will also need to provide your superannuation fund with some paperwork. Give your super fund a call and ask them what they require.

To help you understand how big an opportunity this is, I'll take you through an example.

Case study: David and Julie boost their super by downsizing

David and Julie live in Sydney. They bought their home 25 years ago, have raised their three children in the home, and all three have moved out to start their own independent lives. Having owned their property for so long, David and Julie have paid off the mortgage and find it's now worth $5 million — far more than what they paid for it 25 years ago. David and Julie are in their early 60s and like the idea of living closer to the beach in an apartment that they can just lock-up and leave, as they plan to holiday regularly around Australia and overseas. They also don't need the space nor want to maintain the garden anymore, and have been looking at apartments around the $3 million mark. Here's how David and Julie could use super contribution rules, including downsizing, to their advantage.

David and Julie could sell their house for $5 million and buy an apartment for $3 million. After buy and sell costs, they would have something like $1.6 to $1.7 million left over. David and Julie each have less than $1.76 million in their super (remember non-concessional super contributions from page 127?), so they could both use $360 000 to contribute a total of $720 000 to their superannuation, and then both use the downsizing rules to contribute a further $300 000 each for a total of $600 000.

As a result of the downsize, David and Julie have boosted their combined superannuation by $1.32 million ($720 000 from their non-concessional super contribution + $600,000 from downsize). See figure 7.2 for more details.

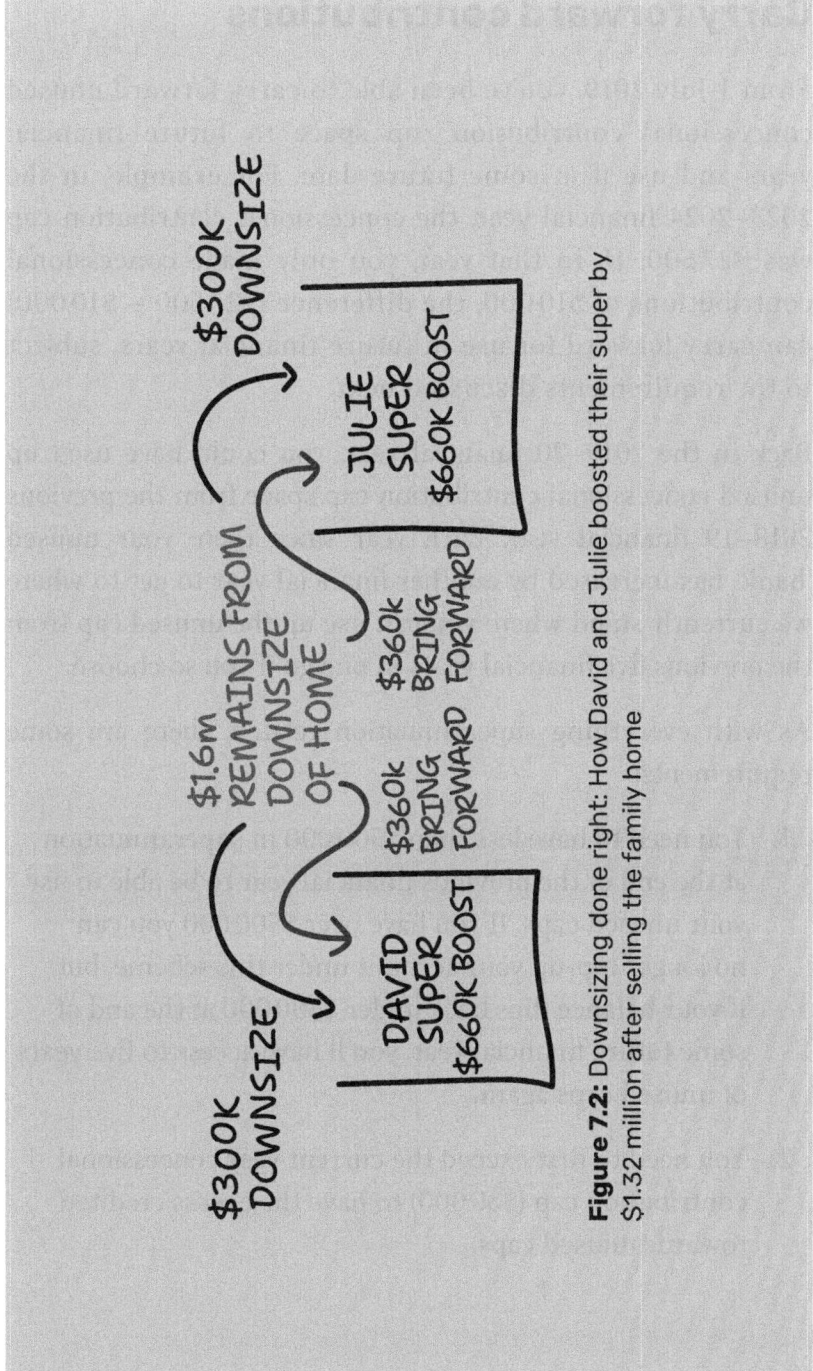

Figure 7.2: Downsizing done right: How David and Julie boosted their super by $1.32 million after selling the family home

Carry forward contributions

From 1 July 2019, you've been able to carry forward unused concessional contribution cap space to future financial years and use it at some future date. For example, in the 2023–2024 financial year, the concessional contribution cap was $27500. If, in that year, you only made concessional contributions of $10000, the difference ($27500 – $10000) can carry forward for use in future financial years, subject to the requirements discussed next.

Back in the 2019–20 financial year, you could have used up unused concessional contribution cap space from the previous 2018–19 financial year. Each year since then, your unused 'bank' has increased by another financial year to get to where we currently stand where you can use up the unused cap from the previous five financial years in one go if you so choose.

As with everything superannuation related, there are some requirements:

1. You need to have less than $500000 in superannuation at the end of the previous financial year to be able to use your unused caps. If you have over $500000 you can no longer top-up your account under this scheme, but if your balance dips back under $500000 at the end of some future financial year, you'll have access to five years of unused caps again.

2. You need to first exceed the current year concessional contribution cap ($30000) to have the excess credited towards unused caps.

3. Your excess above the current year cap is first allocated to the furthest year back where you have unused cap, before then moving forward in a waterfall type fashion to the more recent years.

Case Study : Julie uses her concessional caps

Now that David and Julie have sold their home, let's take a look at how Julie could make these contributions work for her. She had $330 000 in superannuation before she made those contributions from the downsizing ($360 000 from the sale and $300 000 under the downsize rule) and her concessional contributions over the last five years looked like this:

Financial year	Concessional contribution cap	Concessional contributions made	Unused concessional contribution cap space
2019–20	$25 000	$8500	$16 500
2020–21	$25 000	$9000	$16 000
2021–22	$27 500	$9100	$18 400
2022–23	$27 500	$10 200	$17 300
2023–24	$27 500	$10 500	$17 000
Total			$85 200

© Commonwealth of Australia

Note: the concessional contribution cap has increased over the last five years (as mentioned on page 127, the concessional contribution cap at 2025 was $30 000).

(continued)

If we look at this example, Julie has $85 200 (total of the unused concessional contribution cap space) in concessional contributions she could make to superannuation, over and above the current 2024–25 concessional limit of $30 000. Julie could use some of the proceeds from selling her house to make concessional contributions to superannuation, which she would be able to claim as a tax deduction against any other income she might have – her salary from work, for example.

If Julie did make the $300 000 downsizing contribution and the $360 000 non-concessional contribution, her balance would be well above $500 000 by the end of the financial year, so this would be Julie's last opportunity to make use of her carry forward concessional contributions.

This shows how important careful planning of your contributions is as you can lose opportunities if you aren't careful.

Carry forward concessional contributions are a great opportunity for you to top-up your superannuation if you haven't been contributing to the maximum while also creating a nice tax deduction at the same time. Many people use these rules in a year they have additional income from somewhere. Perhaps you sold an investment property and made a big gain; rather than pay quite so much capital gains tax, this allows you to reduce your income down and, as a result, pay less tax on the sale of the property. It all contributes to preparing you for the retirement life you want to live.

Contribution splitting

Among a couple, it's very common for one person to have a lot more in superannuation than the other. Differences in income earned, length of time working in Australia, length of time in the workforce in general, periods of time out of the workforce, or working full-time versus part time all combine to cause these differences.

For a variety of reasons, one I'll tackle here, it doesn't make a great deal of sense for one member of the couple to have a large superannuation balance and one member of the couple to have a smaller balance if it's at all possible to keep them a little more even.

The first reason is to do with the amount you can transfer to a tax-free account-based pension. As I described on page 135, this is currently limited to $2 million, anything in excess of $2 million must remain in accumulation where you will continue to pay tax on the earnings. If, however, you moved some of your contributions over to your spouse's superannuation fund over the years (which, in turn, slows the growth in the balance of your account), that might just be enough to keep you under the $2 million limit. The extra super sits on your spouse's account where they too can commence an account-based pension with up to $2 million once they meet the necessary requirements.

Two people making the best use possible of their $2 million pension cap is much better retirement planning than one person having hundreds of thousands stuck in accumulation while the other has hundreds of thousands of unused pension cap space.

Contribution splitting allows you to split up to 85 per cent of the concessional contributions you have received into your superannuation fund across to your partner's. It's only 85 per cent to allow for the standard 15 per cent tax levied in your superannuation fund on concessional superannuation contributions. After the end of each financial year, you can request that your superannuation fund split contributions received into your superannuation for the year just gone across to your partner's superannuation fund.

As far as the $30 000 concessional contribution caps goes, you received the contribution initially (before electing to split it to your partner), so the contribution counts against your cap. The transfer across to your partner does not count as a contribution for them, nor does it count as a reduction in the available contribution cap space they may have.

So, if both you and your spouse were contributing the maximum $30 000 in annual concessional contributions, and you elected to implement the contribution splitting strategy, your spouse's account could be growing through their own $30 000 contribution, which, after allowing for the 15 per cent tax, becomes $25 500; and a contribution split from you, being 85 per cent of the $30 000 you contributed to your own superannuation fund (or $25 500), which totals $51 000. And, on top of that, there is the investment earnings on their account.

Since you've moved the contributions received into your account across to your partner's account, their account will grow quite quickly with the combination of contributions and investment earnings, while your account will grow by just investment earnings.

When I've suggested this strategy to couples over the years, some people ask: 'But wouldn't the compounding on a bigger account be better than spreading some money to a smaller account?' That's not how the maths works. If a $1 million account earned 10 per cent return, that equals $100 000. If, instead, there was an $800 000 account and a $200 000 account that each earned 10 per cent return, they would each earn $80 000 and $20 000 respectively. Add the two accounts together (to get the $1 million value) and the returns are the same $80 000 + $20 000 = $100 000.

Spouse contribution

A spouse contribution, as the name suggests, is a contribution you make to your spouse's superannuation fund. A spouse contribution counts towards the receiving spouse's non-concessional ($120 000) contribution limit. So, in order to make a spouse contribution, your spouse first needs to be eligible to make a non-concessional contribution, as I discussed back on page 127.

Spouse contributions are particularly beneficial if the receiving spouse is a low income earner, earning under $37 000. If the receiving spouse earns under $37 000, the contributing spouse can make a contribution to their spouse's superannuation fund and receive a $540 tax offset for the first $3000 contributed. Contributing anything more than $3000 doesn't provide any further offset, the maximum offset is $540.

The tax offset benefit starts to reduce if your spouse earns more than $37 000. The benefit phases out for income between $37 000 and $40 000; above $40 000 there is no tax offset benefit.

Superannuation co-contribution

The superannuation co-contribution scheme is a government-funded superannuation contribution-matching scheme designed to encourage lower income earners to add some of their own money to superannuation. If you meet the income tests described here, the government will add $0.50 to your superannuation fund for every dollar of non-concessional contribution you make up to a maximum of $500 government contribution for the first $1000 non-concessional contribution you make.

The two main income requirements are:

1. more than 10 per cent of your income earned must come from employment or running a business

2. your income must be below $45 400. Between $45 400 and $60 400 the benefit phases out, before it stops completely above $60 400.

I see the co-contribution strategy used a lot by parents who have children just entering the workforce. Perhaps the child has a part-time job while at school or university, and it's unlikely the child would be earning more than $45 400 so the parent gives the child $1000 to deposit into their superannuation fund and the government will chip in a top-up of $500. Do this during their younger years and let the magic of time and compound returns do their thing for the next 40 years — you'll have given your child a nice kick to their retirement savings.

Defined benefit funds

Although very uncommon these days, there are still many people around who have their superannuation in a defined benefit fund. If that's you (if you have a defined benefit fund, you know you have a defined benefit fund), then a lot of what I've explained to this point about superannuation isn't a whole lot relevant to you. If your defined benefit fund doesn't offer a lifetime pension option, then the account-based pension section on page 133 will be relevant to you.

You see, the balance of a defined benefit fund, as the name suggests, is 'defined' by a formula rather than the amount you have contributed and the return earned on those contributions. The formula that determines the balance of your superannuation will be some combination of a range of factors, typically they include:

- length of service

- your average salary over the last three or five years of your working life

- some multiplication factor that increases the longer you work for the company.

Members of defined benefit funds are still subject to the same contribution limits everyone else is, it's just that, rather than actual dollars being added to their account, there's a 'notional' amount of the increase in their account balance counted as a contribution. If that notional amount is less than the contribution limits I described previously, then you can add more of your own contributions to superannuation if you like.

Given the balance of your account is defined by a formula, your account is not exposed to the ups and downs of investment markets, nor do you have to worry about picking an investment option (unless you also have an accumulation account that you're adding money to). This can be both good and bad. There will be periods of time where investment markets perform really well, possibly better than the increase in your balance as a result of the defined benefit formula. There will also be periods of time where investment markets perform poorly, and you are not exposed to that in a defined benefit fund as your balance is determined by the formula.

While defined benefit funds all operate on a somewhat similar formula, they all have their slight differences. If you do have a defined benefit fund and you need some help planning your options, it's best to start with getting some advice from the benefit provider. They all employ financial advisers who know their particular employer's fund inside out, so it's a good start. If not there, please make sure you ask a financial adviser what their experience is working with defined benefit providers.

Defined benefit funds are not only different to accumulation funds in the building up stage, they also tend to be different in the retirement/pension phase. You'll typically have two options with your defined benefit fund when it comes to retirement:

1. Your benefit is converted to a lump sum that you can either roll over to an ordinary accumulation-style superannuation fund and convert into an account-based pension, or withdraw some or all of your benefit from the superannuation system entirely as a cash withdrawal.

2. You can convert some or all of your benefit to a lifetime pension. This may pay a fixed amount to you for the rest

of your life; it may be indexed in line with inflation once or twice a year; and it may pay some form of reversionary pension to your partner should you die before they do (often at a reduced amount to that which was paid to you).

Sometimes you can elect any combination of these two options. Half lump sum, half lifetime pension; 20 per cent lump sum and 80 per cent lifetime pension; or any other combination they allow. Get some help from a financial adviser who has dealt with this type of benefit before.

Finally, tax on defined benefit funds — again, this depends on the provider. Some defined benefits will pay you a tax-free lump sum or pension upon retirement, and with others, there's tax you'll have to pay. Sometimes the payment you receive from a defined benefit fund is taxed as ordinary income for the remainder of your life, with a small tax offset. They all vary so it's important you understand how your particular defined benefit works, if you have one.

Annuities

Annuities are a way for people with ordinary accumulation-style superannuation accounts (or even money that isn't inside superannuation) to invest a portion of their retirement savings with a guarantee to receive an income payment for the rest of their life. As I touched on earlier in this chapter, account-based pensions and TRIS (the two most common form of superannuation retirement income streams) have no guarantee that you will continue to receive payments through your lifetime. If you spend a lot or don't earn enough in terms of returns, you may outlive your account-based pension.

With an annuity, you exchange a lump sum of money for a guaranteed income stream for the rest of your life. There are many different types of annuities — similar to a defined benefit, this is another area where you are likely to need some help. Depending on the type of annuity you select, you may receive a flat payment for the rest of your life, it could be indexed by some percentage, or it may have some form of investment market exposure so your payments may go up and down a little from year to year (with a guarantee of at least a minimum payment each year).

Some annuities will allow you to withdraw back some of your initial investment for a period of time (which, in turn, will reduce your income payments); for others, there is no access to your capital once you commence receiving payments. Some you can purchase at any time, and defer receiving payments until some future date.

The various options available almost seem endless. For many years, there was next to no innovation in the space of annuities. But from 1 July 2019, the government changed how they assess lifetime annuities for Services Australia income and asset test purposes, and also pushed the industry to come up with new ways of dealing with longevity risk (the risk that you run out of money before you die). The changes to the Services Australia assessment meant you could get more age pension by using a lifetime annuity than you would otherwise receive having all of your superannuation in an account-based pension.

As you can imagine, the combination of increased aged pension benefits (or in some cases, qualifying to get an age pension when you otherwise wouldn't have been able to), together with the guarantee of an income stream for the rest of your life has proven to be very attractive to many people. Since 1 July 2019, there has been a noticeable increase in the number of people using annuities and, as a consequence, there has been renewed innovation in the space.

There's a lot to think about in this chapter, all of which will help you design a superannuation strategy to boost and support your ideal retirement life. Seeking some professional help when navigating superannuation can be of incredible value to you. Most superannuation funds offer free or heavily subsidised financial advice about superannuation or you could speak with a financial adviser who doesn't work for one of the super funds. Either way, this chapter hopefully leaves you armed with some knowledge that will enable you to ask the right questions and feel assured your super is doing its job for your future so you can retire life ready.

Retire life ready steps

Work out where all your superannuation is, what investment options you have and what their past performance has been like. Are you using the right investment option for your current stage of life?

Would a financial adviser help you navigate your superannuation strategy and investment choice?

Can you afford to add anything more to superannuation that may save you some tax and boost your retirement savings?

Is there any benefit for you in a spouse contribution, contribution splitting or a co-contribution?

Can you use any of the more advanced super strategies around downsizing or trying to eliminate the inheritance tax burden as you get towards retirement or beyond?

CHAPTER 8
Ensuring you can get there with insurance

No-one likes to pay for insurance, but in the event you need it, you're going to be glad you have it.

I can almost guarantee the car you drive is insured, your home is likely insured as is the contents of your home, but what about your biggest asset? Is that insured?

For most people, particularly those reading this who are in their 30s and 40s, their biggest asset is their ability to earn an income. Think about what you earn today, then multiply that by the next 20 or 30 years of working life you might have ahead of you. Allow some for the pay rises coming your way, and very quickly we are talking many millions of dollars. You insure your $50 000 car, but have you insured the millions of dollars of earnings capacity you have ahead of you?

My view on insurance is that it should be used to plug the gap between where you are now and where you are aspiring to be and nothing more — don't pay for things you don't need. As you've worked through this book, you have calculated exactly how much you need to retire with the lifestyle you want. In Chapter 2, you worked out where you are now, and in Chapter 3, you worked out how much you need for retirement. Since then, we've been working to close that gap.

The first thing those plans to close the gap rely on is you being alive; the second is you being able to earn an income. If you aren't here, or you can't earn an income, you won't ever close the gap. Insurance should be used to close that gap.

There are four types of personal insurances I want you to understand. The intricacies of each type of policy is beyond the scope of this book, but I want to leave you with enough information to know that you need to find out more. Each type of insurance can play a role in preparing you financially for your retired life.

Within each type of policy, there are a wide variety of premium structures and features on offer from each of the insurance companies that operate in the Australian market. I highly encourage you to get expert advice in this area, don't just rely on the default cover that comes from your superannuation fund. It's often like comparing oranges and apples.

1. Income protection

Statistically, income protection is the most likely insurance policy you may claim on. During their working lives, many people find themselves unable to work for a period of time, often due to sickness or injury, and without enough sick leave or other entitlements, you can easily find yourself in a position where your employer puts you on leave without pay.

Under an income protection policy, you need to be off work for a pre-determined length of time (although you might still be being paid by your employer via sick leave, for example), known as the *waiting period*, before the insurance company will start to pay you. The shorter the waiting period you select, the more expensive your income protection policy will be.

Once you are 'on claim', the insurance company will pay you the monthly benefit you are covered for. This might be something like 70 per cent of your pre-disability income. Income protection payments are taxable income, so remember to put some aside to cover the tax bill you will have once you lodge your tax return.

As long as you are unable to go back to work, the insurance company will continue to pay you for the duration of what's called the *benefit period*. The benefit period is a period of time you selected when you took out the income protection policy that the insurance company will pay you for. This might be as little as two years or it might be right up until you turn 65. The longer you choose, the more expensive your income protection policy will be.

Remember, without your ability to earn an income, you have next to no chance of closing the gap between where you are today and where you need to be to retire life ready — so take your income protection policy seriously.

2. Life insurance

Lots of people worry about having life insurance and, sure, we all know someone who died well before they should have, but life insurance is the policy you are least likely to claim on.

Pre-existing conditions and family history aside, you are likely to live well into your 80s. The insurance companies know this, so on a dollar premium versus dollar insurance benefit basis, life insurance is the cheapest policy you can take out. It's also a fairly simple policy: you are either dead or you are alive. (It does get a little more complicated than that in that most life insurance policies will pay out if a couple of doctors sign off to say you are unlikely to live more than two years.)

While you are unlikely to claim on a life insurance policy, the ramifications of you dying without one can be catastrophic for those you leave behind. Those you leave behind will inherit your assets as well as your liabilities. Perhaps you're leaving a partner and children behind, what position are they in to carry on paying the debts (mortgage, bills, school fees etc.) without you around?

The same applies if you are single: Think about what you are leaving behind and to who you are leaving it. Do you want to leave those assets with the debts paid off or are you comfortable that someone inherits everything and the inheritor sorts it all out?

3. Total and permanent disability insurance

Often linked to a life insurance policy (particularly if your life insurance policy is held through superannuation) is total and permanent disability insurance (TPD for short). Like the name suggests, TPD pays out in the event you are unlikely to ever be able to work again.

Like the other insurances I've discussed to this point, there are differences and options in the policy you can select.

One type of TPD policy will pay out in the event you can't do your 'own' occupation. That is, the insurance company takes on the liability that you may only be injured to an extent that you can't do the job you are insured for. You may still be capable of doing a different job, but that doesn't matter. Under an 'own' occupation TPD policy, if you can't do your job, you'll be paid out your insurance.

The other type of TPD policy is known as an 'any' occupation. Under an 'any' occupation policy, the insurance company will only pay out if you are unable to work in a job you are suitable for given your education, training and experience. It might not be your current job, but if you are capable of doing another job related to your skills, the insurance company won't pay you out.

Depending on how you own your TPD policy (inside of superannuation or not), the tax implications of a payout can vary wildly. Please seek professional advice on setting one of these policies up correctly.

4. Trauma insurance

The final major insurance policy you should have to cover you is trauma insurance. Trauma insurance pays out in the event of a 'traumatic' event. The different insurance companies will have a list of events that are covered, and they won't all be the same events.

The major events that people claim on these policies are heart attack, stroke and cancer. There are many other claimable events, but these three seem to be the most common claims.

Trauma insurance pays a tax-free lump sum to you in the event you suffer a claimable event. Typically, the event means a length of time off work and some medical bills and a recovery period. We use trauma insurance to cover these events.

I've seen some clients with huge trauma policies, enough to pay out their mortgage. Trauma insurance is quite costly, so we'd rather not have massive sums insured, and leave the life and TPD insurance to cover things like the mortgage. But again, please seek advice on your unique circumstances.

Claiming on multiple policies

With the four types of insurance I've described here, it's possible for you to claim one event on multiple policies.

Say, for example, you have a stroke. You are able to immediately claim on your trauma insurance. If, while you are recovering from your stroke, you are off work for long enough to cover your waiting period on your income protection policy, that policy will start to pay out. Perhaps it was a serious stroke, and it becomes apparent that you aren't recovering enough to be able to return to work, so you may then be able to claim on your TPD policy.

While an extreme example, it does provide a scenario where you claim on trauma, followed by income protection and then TPD. Even after you've claimed on your TPD policy, your income protection will continue to pay you monthly until the end of your benefit period (if you never return to work).

Client story: Retiring life ready on insurance payments

I recently did some work for a client in their early 50s, who, in his early 40s, suffered a fall. The fall meant he hasn't been able to work since. Fortunately, when he was in his 30s and had his first child, he sought some advice to ensure he had an appropriate level of insurances in place.

Given the insurances he had, he was able to claim on both his TPD insurance and his income protection. The income protection paid at such a level that the family was comfortably able to continue living and paying the mortgage, and so while he claimed on his TPD insurance, he hasn't pulled money out of his superannuation.

Now, in his early 50s, he has in excess of $3 million in his superannuation fund as a result of continued contributions (made from his income protection payments) and the TPD payout. When the income protection payments eventually stop after he turns 65, his superannuation balance will be significantly more, but most importantly, he will be able to fund a very comfortable income for the remainder of his life and leave a sizeable inheritance to his daughter.

No-one likes to pay for insurance, particularly when you think that you are paying for something you really hope doesn't happen to you. In the case of the insurances discussed here, it's likely to be some quite serious health event that enables you to claim — not something anyone really wants to have happen. But, remember, insurance is added protection to ensure that magic number of net nest egg assets isn't derailed by life events. It's about protecting your wealth and protecting your path to build that wealth, so you can live your dream life well past your working years.

Retire life ready steps

Consider what would happen to you and your family if you were unable to work anymore. What would happen to the life you know today? What would happen to the plans you are building to enable you to retire life ready. Without your ability to earn an income, the lifestyle you enjoy today may stop.

Look up your superannuation fund and write down what amounts you have for the following insurances:

- Life $_____

- Total and permanent disability $_____

- Income protection $_____

How long do you need to be off work before you are paid your income protection? _____

How long will your income protection be paid for? _____

Do you have any additional amounts you are paying towards insurance outside of your superannuation fund? If yes, how much? $_____

Do you hold a trauma or critical illness insurance policy? If so, how much is it for? $_____

Looking at the numbers you have listed here, how long would you or your family be able to continue your current lifestyle for under these policies?_____

Will this leave you short on your net nest egg asset number?

Consider whether you and your family need more protecting than what you already have in place, or are you appropriately covered so you can live comfortably and meet your retirement goals with what you have in place already.

CHAPTER 9
The age pension and more

If superannuation is the backbone of your retirement, the age pension is your safety net. Some people feel that because they have paid taxes during their working lives, they ought to be entitled to an age pension. That's not how it works here in Australia. The age pension is a safety net for those who don't have enough financial resources to support themselves in retirement. It's not a guaranteed entitlement for everyone. The government simply cannot afford to pay everyone an age pension.

Getting an age pension is towards the top of the goals list for many people I meet with. I explain to them that, if you are able to, you are far better off having your own money and not qualifying for an age pension than you are having less money and relying on the age pension. Having your own money gives you the flexibility to do what you want when you want, and spend as much as you want, rather than being at the mercy of a fortnightly payment from Services Australia.

I'd love you to be excited about the prospect of *not* getting an age pension because you've done so much amazing work to build your net nest egg assets number to where you are truly self-sufficient. The age pension will be there if you need it, but if you start early enough, plan and execute on that plan, you can be fully in control of your retirement.

If your asset position come retirement means you are likely to get some form of age pension, maybe a part pension, then doing all you can to optimise your retirement savings to maximise what you can get in an age pension is a great idea. Clients with asset levels that mean they get a part age pension are some of my happiest clients in retirement.

Just be aware that the rules around qualifying for an age pension can change. For example, back in 2015, legislation was passed to change the way the taper rate for the asset test (explained on page 196) worked. The changes implemented from 1 July 2017, increased the lower threshold of the asset test, which gave more people with lower assets a full age pension. But they also doubled the rate at which your age pension was reduced if your assets exceeded the lower threshold. This meant that a number of people with assets towards the upper end of the old asset test limit had their age pensions cut off completely.

I had a number of clients impacted by these changes at the time. They were receiving a part age pension and had set up their retirement plans around that, only to have their age pension cut off because their assets were above the revised asset limits. To say they were unhappy would be an understatement. Almost ten years later, one of my clients still talks about how unfair he thinks it was to be working towards one set of rules as he approached retirement only to have them significantly change on him a few years into retirement. I understand where he's coming from, but as I already mentioned, your eligibility for the age pension is not guaranteed, and if the government of the day needs to make changes, it will.

If you're in your 40s and you're reading this book, I think it would be foolish for you to be relying on an age pension to supplement your retirement. As the Australian population ages, and we have less working Australians and more in retirement, there will be increasing pressure on the government to try and balance the budget as best it can. I think it's inevitable that age pension entitlements will be reduced further. We'll always have an age pension, but don't expect it to look like it does today in 20 years from now.

As you prepare to retire life ready there are two Services Australia entitlements that you need to know about:

1. age pension

2. health care card benefits.

Let's explore the benefits of each and how you qualify.

The age pension

As you may well be aware, the age pension pays you a fortnightly entitlement and it comes with the pension concession card. Your fortnightly entitlement is based on two tests: the income test and the asset test.

I'll explain these two tests in a moment, but for now, just know that Services Australia assesses your financial position using both tests. The more assets you have or the higher your income, the less age pension you will be paid. The test that results in the lowest rate of payment is the payment you will receive.

As Figure 9.1 (overleaf) shows, there's a maximum amount of pension you can receive that then tapers off as your income or assets increase, until you eventually get no age pension.

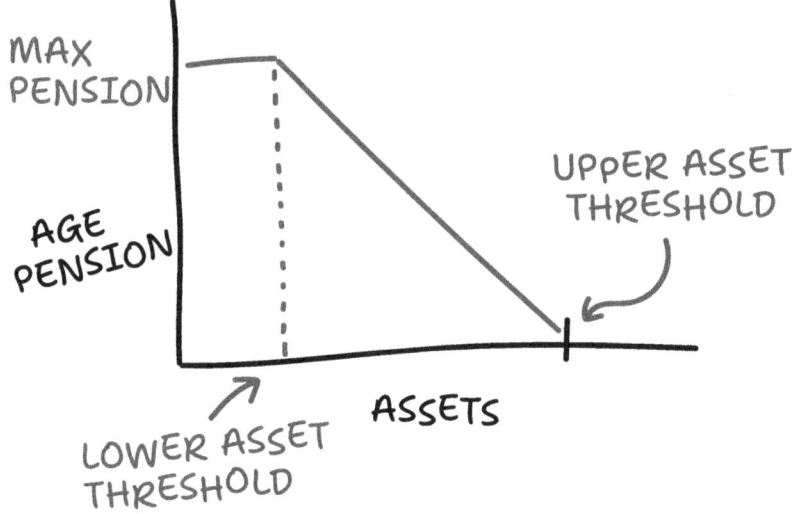

Figure 9.1: Understanding the income and asset thresholds: How the age pension tapers

The first step in qualifying for an age pension is you need to be old enough. That age currently stands at age 67, and at the time of writing, there are no plans for that to increase. Again, if you are 40 years old, don't expect to get an age pension at 67, it will probably be a higher age by the time you get there.

The second step is you need to be here in Australia to claim your age pension. For the vast majority of people claiming an age pension, this part isn't an issue. It can be an issue for you though if you've spent time living outside of Australia just before you turn 67 or if it's your intention to collect your age pension and then go and live overseas. While it is possible to continue to have your Australian age pension paid to you if you are living in another country, it can be complicated, and my best advice would be for you to contact Services Australia to discuss your unique situation.

Age pension payment rates are indexed up every six months: on 20 March and again on 20 September each year. Following are the maximum payment rates at the time of writing (January 2025), but given the frequency with which these rates increase, it would be best for you to visit servicesaustralia.gov.au to understand what the payment rates are at the time you're reading this.

Per fortnight	Single	Couple each	Couple combined	Couple apart due to ill health
Maximum basic rate	$1047.10	$789.30	$1578.60	$1047.10
Maximum pension supplement	$83.20	$62.70	$125.40	$83.20
Energy supplement	$14.10	$10.60	$21.20	$14.10
Total	$1144.40	$862.60	$1725.20	$1144.40

Source: © Commonwealth of Australia.

A couple of things to note from this table:

- Think of the maximum pension supplement and energy supplement as top-ups to your pension. These are amounts the government can change or remove much more easily than they can the rate of age pension. These two supplements are also payable as soon as you qualify for even $1 of fortnightly age pension. So the lowest fortnightly entitlement you might receive as a single person is $83.20 (pension supplement) + $14.10 (energy supplement) = $97.30.

- A single person is paid more age pension than each individual member of a couple. This is to account for it

not costing twice as much to run a household of two than it does one.

- If, as part of a couple, one of you is age pension age and the other isn't, assuming your combined income and assets mean you would qualify for a pension, the person who is old enough will be paid their entitlement based on the couple rate (that is one half of their couple entitlement). When the younger person is old enough, they, too, will be paid their entitlement based on the couple rate.

- A couple apart due to ill health is most commonly one person in aged care and one person still living at home. They receive the single-person payment rate, which is higher than the rate for each individual member of a couple.

Age pension income test

Under the income test your (and your partner's, if you have one), income from all sources is assessed by Services Australia. This includes income you might earn from work as well as income from financial assets, such as savings, shares, property and superannuation.

Income from work is simple, Services Australia count what you earn, and you'll typically have to report what you earn from work every 14 days.

Income from financial investments, such as savings, shares and superannuation, is assessed under the *deeming rules*. Under the deeming rules, Services Australia doesn't care what interest or return you actually earn on your money, they deem you to earn a particular amount instead. At the time of writing, the deeming rates are still low as a carryover from the low interest rates we had during COVID. They were supposed to increase as of 1 July 2024, but the government postponed the increase for another year. Now that interest rates are starting to fall in Australia, the deeming rates might not get increased — we'll have to wait and see. As with age pension payment rates, you should check the deeming rates at the time you are assessing your eligibility for any Services Australia or age pension benefits. However, at the time of writing the deeming rates are:

- For a single person, the first $62 600 of your financial assets are deemed to earn 0.25 per cent. Anything over $62 600 is deemed to earn 2.25 per cent.

- For a couple, the first $103 800 of your combined financial assets are deemed to earn 0.25 per cent. Anything over $103 800 is deemed to earn 2.25 per cent.

This step-up in percentage rates is designed to account for you having some money in an ordinary transaction account that likely earns very little interest at all, then having the balance of your money in either high interest savings accounts or invested.

If you earn rental income, that's assessed differently to the deeming rate. Somewhat similar to your tax return, Services Australia assesses the gross rental income you earn less some allowable deductions. However, the deductions they allow you to take off the rental income you earn are different to what you would claim in your tax return. If the income you earn less the allowable deductions is negative (turn back to Chapter 5 for more on negative gearing), Services Australia just counts the income as zero. You cannot offset the loss on your investment property against other income when it comes to Services Australia benefits.

You can reduce your gross rental income for Services Australia assessment by:

- interest charged on borrowed money to purchase the property

- rates

- costs to maintain the property.

You'd typically be able to claim the following as deductions in a tax return, but you cannot claim them to reduce your rental income for a Services Australia assessment:

- depreciation

- special building write-off

- cost to build

- costs of borrowing money such as loan establishment fees.

Once you've got the total of your income, it then gets assessed against the following.

For a single person:

Income per fortnight	Amount your pension will reduce by
Up to $212 (free area)	$0
Over $212	50 cents for each dollar over $212

Source: © Commonwealth of Australia.

For a couple:

Combined income per fortnight	Amount each member of the couple's pension will reduce by
Up to $372 (free area)	$0
Over $372	25 cents for each dollar over $372

Source: © Commonwealth of Australia.

You'll be cut off from qualifying for the age pension under the income test if your fortnightly income exceeds these numbers.

Your situation	Fortnightly income cut-off point
Single	$2500.80
Couple living together	$3822.40 combined
Couple living apart due to ill health	$4949.60 combined

Source: © Commonwealth of Australia.

That's just over $65 000 pa for a single person and almost $100 000 for a couple.

The good thing is, you don't need to remember all of this or try to work it out for yourself. Some very smart people have built online calculators that you can plug your details into and get an estimate of your age pension entitlement. I like the one on Noel Whittaker's website (noelwhittaker.com.au).

Age pension asset test

The age pension asset test, as the name suggests, measures the assets you have to support yourself in retirement. The fewer assets you have, the more age pension you will receive (until you are eventually being paid the full age pension). At the other end, the more assets you have, the less age pension you will receive (until your assets are high enough that you get no age pension).

The asset test captures everything you own, except for the value of the home you live in. So things like home contents, cars, boats, caravans, holiday home, investment property, savings, shares, super, jewellery, private companies, trusts — the list goes on — all get counted. Services Australia assess everything. You are even required to disclose assets you own overseas.

You'll notice I said 'everything you own, except for the value of the home you live in'. There are two testing thresholds Services Australia use when they are looking at your assets: one for those who are homeowners and one for those who aren't. Those who don't own their own home are allowed to have an additional level of assets above those who do own their own home, before their age pension entitlements start being reduced or completely cut off. This additional level of assets is to recognise that, if you don't own your own home, you will likely have to pay rent, and as such, have a higher ongoing cost to your retirement than someone who does own their own home.

As a side note: If you are renting in retirement or live in an over-50s retirement community and you qualify for an aged pension, you will be paid rent assistance by Services Australia over and above your age pension entitlements. You just need to qualify for an age pension.

So, what are the extra assets that a non homeowner is allowed? They are allowed $252 000. That's it — $252 000. All other things being equal, you are likely better off owning your own home, if you can afford to do so, and being assessed under the homeowner asset test. Your total assets (value of your home included) can be far higher if you own your own home, while still allowing you to collect an age pension.

Like with the age pension payments themselves, the asset thresholds for qualifying for an age pension are increased in March and September each year. So, look up the tables at servicesaustralia.gov.au at the time this becomes relevant to you. However, at the time of writing, you'll get a full age pension if your assets are below the numbers in the following table. This is known as the lower threshold:

Your situation	Homeowner	Non-homeowner
Single	$314 000	$566 000
Couple, combined	$470 000	$722 000
Couple, separated due to illness, combined	$470 000	$722 000

Source: © Commonwealth of Australia.

You will be cut off from being paid any age pension if your assets exceed those in the following table. This is known as the upper threshold:

Your situation	Homeowner	Non-homeowner
Single	$695 500	$947 500
Couple, combined	$1 045 500	$1 297 500
Couple, separated due to illness, combined	$1 233 000	$1 485 000
Couple, one partner eligible, combined	$1 045 500	$1 297 500

Source: © Commonwealth of Australia.

For every $1000 your assets are above the lower threshold, your fortnightly age pension reduces by $3 for a single person or couple combined.

Strategy tip: If you are part of a couple, with one member of the couple over age pension age (67) and one under, be careful of your superannuation arrangements. If you are under age pension age and your superannuation benefits are in pension mode, the value of your superannuation pension account will be assessed for your partner's age pension entitlements. However, if you are under age pension age and your superannuation benefits aren't in pension mode, they are exempt from assessment by Services Australia.

This provides an opportunity for some couples to move money into the younger person's superannuation fund, where the balance isn't assessed by Services Australia. This may result in the older member of the couple being paid a higher rate of age pension for a period of time. Eventually, the younger person will be age pension age and their super will count too, so this strategy will only work for a period of time, but it's certainly worth exploring if there's an age gap between you and your partner.

As mentioned, I would suggest you just use one of the online calculators to get an estimate of your age pension entitlement. That's what I do when I'm doing come client work involving the age pension.

I think it's really important as you plan to retire life ready, that you understand how much the age pension pays (it's not a terribly large amount of money on its own) and have an idea of the level of assets required to qualify for a full or part age pension. If you're a younger person reading this book, it will help put some perspective on your spending and net nest egg numbers to see how much you need to be self-sufficient.

Low income health care card

At the beginning of this chapter, I mentioned that I have many clients who aspire to get the age pension. I tend to challenge people on that, show them what the age pension pays and how often, and we look at how far that is away from the type of retirement they are aspiring to lead.

What I find a lot of people want is the pension concession card, not necessarily the age pension payments. They hope to live off more than the age pension so can appreciate they will need significant assets to do that. If that's you, you'll want to know about the low income health care card. As the name suggests, this is a health care card for people with low incomes (not necessarily low assets, which I'll get to shortly) that provides many (but not quite all) of the benefits that the pension concession card gets you, including:

- access to the Pharmaceutical Benefits Scheme (PBS) for cheap prescription medications

- discount on council rates (some councils)

- discount off energy bills (some states)

- discount car registration (some states).

A lot of the benefits of the low income health care card vary from state to state, so it's best to check with your local Services Australia branch about what you can use the card for where you live. If you get the low income health care card, make it a habit to ask everywhere if they accept it so you can make best use of the card.

Unlike claiming the age pension, there is no minimum age requirement for qualifying for the low income health care card. You could be 45 years old and, if your income and assets are such that you meet the income test, you can get the card.

The income test is similar to that of the age pension. Various different sources of income are all added up, including things like (but not limited to):

- salary, wages, self-employment income

- employer fringe benefits

- rental income

- reportable super contributions

- deeming on financial assets.

Your financial assets, things like cash savings, shares and superannuation pension benefits are deemed in the same way that deeming works for the age pension (see page 166 for more on deemed assets).

All of your income plus deeming is added up and then assessed against the following limits. At the time of writing, your income needs to be below these thresholds at the time you apply for the card and then again when it comes up for renewal. There is a bit of grace given to you for your income to fluctuate upwards while you hold the card, but come renewal time, it must be back down below these thresholds.

Status	Weekly income	Income in an eight-week period
Single, no children	$783.00	$6264.00
Couple combined, no children	$1339.00	$10 712.00
Single, one dependent child	$1339.00	$10 712.00
Couple combined, one child	$1373.00	$10 984.00
For each extra child, add	$34.00	$272.00

Source: © Commonwealth of Australia.

So, a single person would need to have income below $40 716 and a couple have income below $69 628 to qualify for the low income health care card. You might recall back in Chapter 2, I discussed ASFA's retirement income standard and what they suggested a couple needs for a comfortable retirement. ASFA's assessment of the income required for a comfortable retirement is more than these low income health care card thresholds.

However, if you've set yourself up properly for retirement and taken advantage of the superannuation system as best you can, then the money you spend funding your retirement can be far greater than those limits and you can still get the low income health care card.

What? Let me explain.

You see, if you have the bulk of your money to fund retirement sitting inside of the superannuation system paying you a tax-free pension, Services Australia doesn't care how much you pay out to yourself to live off as income. Services Australia doesn't factor what you take from super to live off into their assessment of your eligibility for this card. All Services Australia care about is their deeming assessment of your account balance.

Now because deeming rates are still so low, a single person could have just over $1.8 million in a tax-free account-based pension, and Services Australia's deeming calculation would say their income is below $40 716, so they qualify for the low income health care card. However, even though the minimum superannuation pension draw-down rates that superannuation pension would need to pay out are about $72 000 per annum tax free (you could be taking more if you wanted), you would still meet the definition of low income for this health care card because Services Australia does not count your superannuation payments.

In a similar scenario, a couple could have just over $3 million in combined tax-free account-based pensions and have Services Australia assess their deemed income under $69 628. Those account-based pensions would need to pay out minimum pension payments of at least $120000 per annum (combined) tax free to the couple, but they would still meet the income threshold for this health care card.

Both the single person and the couple have retirement incomes well above ASFA's comfortable retirement number. As you can see, with the right structuring, you can have quite a healthy retirement savings balance and still get some level of support from Services Australia.

Commonwealth seniors health card

The final benefit in the list of common Services Australia entitlements that you may qualify for is the Commonwealth seniors health card. If I ranked the three Services Australia benefits I've discussed in order of most support to least support, the age pension and the pension concession card that comes with it would be the first on the list, followed by the low income health care card. This card comes third.

The main benefit of getting this card, is access to the PBS for cheap prescription medications. It has a far higher income threshold than the low income health care card so a lot more people can qualify for this card. Outside of accessing the PBS, there aren't a whole lot of other benefits recipients of this card receive. But, as with my suggestion for the low income health care card, you're best to try everywhere to see if they will accept the card to get the most out of it.

One somewhat quirky entitlement with this card that you don't typically get on the low income health care card is a cash payment if the government decides to stimulate the economy. If you remember back to COVID, for example, the Australian Government handed out cash to different groups within the Australian population to help them through that time. If you had the Commonwealth seniors health card, you received the cash payment; however, if you only had the low income health care card you didn't get the payment.

I always found that strange because you need to have lower means to get the low income health care card than you do the Commonwealth seniors health card, but the government decided to give the payments to one card holder and not the other. I'm not sure why they did that.

All of my clients with a Commonwealth seniors health card received cash payments during COVID. Many of them commented: 'I don't understand why I get this money, I don't need it.' They were retired, not worried about losing their jobs or having to juggle working from home while helping children with online schooling (wasn't that fun), and had more than enough assets that they didn't need the $700. It was amazing to see so many of my clients give that $700 to others in their life or community that they felt needed it more. It made me feel so proud to have played a part in securing the financial stability of these clients so they could then give to those who needed it more.

The good news for you is that if you meet the income test for both the low income and the Commonwealth seniors cards, you can have both. I always suggest you get both if you can qualify for them because, just like the cash handouts I described, one card will give you some benefits and the other might give you other benefits. Sometimes Services Australia gets confused if you apply for both, but you can definitely have both if you qualify.

The Commonwealth seniors health card has a minimum age requirement. Just like the age pension, you can't get this card until you are 67. If you're younger, apply for the low income health care card, and then when you turn 67, apply for the Commonwealth seniors health card.

Your income for this card is assessed differently to both the age pension and the low income health care card. For the Commonwealth seniors card, they use something called *adjusted taxable income*, and you can use your income from either of the two financial years prior to the current year in your application. You use details off your tax return (if you've lodged one) to complete the application. If you haven't lodged a tax return because your income is too low, then you put the details of the income you did earn.

The income calculation looks like this:

> **Taxable income**
> **+ Foreign income**
> **+ Net rental property loss**
> **+ Net financial investment loss**
> **+ Value of employer provided benefits above $1000**
> **+ Reportable super contributions**
> **+ Personal deductible super contributions**

As you can see, you can't use negative gearing on investments or tax-deductible super contributions to reduce your income for this card. Those deductions are added back to your income.

The final consideration is deeming on account-based pension funds using the same deeming rules explained on page 166. Interestingly, for the Commonwealth seniors health card, money you have in superannuation in the accumulation phase (so it's not paying you a pension) is not counted for the income test. That may be a strategic opportunity for you if getting a health care card is particularly valuable to you and your income, or your assets are at a level where, if you had all your superannuation paying pensions, you wouldn't get the card.

The income test for this card increased significantly a few years ago and currently stands at:

- $99 025 a year if you're single

- $158 440 a year for couples

- $198 050 a year for couples separated by illness, respite or prison.

Given how high those limits are, the vast majority of retirees over the age of 67 will be eligible for this card. Similar to our discussion about the low income health care card on page 172, if you've done a great job maximising your usage of the superannuation system, a single person could have around $4.4 million in superannuation (if they weren't earning any other income elsewhere) and still get this card. For a couple that increases to $7 million and an illness-separated couple $8.8 million — that's some serious retirement savings.

Most retirees get some income support

Around 63 per cent of people over the age of 65 receive some income support from the government. As we get closer and closer to a time when people have had the benefit of the superannuation system for their whole working lives, this number will likely decrease as retirement savings balances, on average, will be higher than in previous generations.

The age pension alone doesn't provide the type of retirement most people aspire to, but as I've mentioned, funding a retirement with a part age pension and part your own assets provides a very comfortable retirement for many.

Perhaps, in the earlier chapters, you've mapped out a retirement spending number that requires net nest egg assets well above what would allow you even a part age pension. You hopefully now have an appreciation that, even with higher levels of assets in retirement, you can still get a level of support through the health care card system.

Retire life ready steps

As you can see, assistance in retirement from Services Australia extends beyond just the age pension. You can have many millions of dollars in superannuation, live a very, very comfortable retirement and still qualify for some level of support.

While I encouraged you at the beginning of the chapter to be excited by the prospect of being self-sufficient in retirement and not receive an age pension, I am a big advocate of you doing all you can to structure your affairs so you can get whatever assistance you may be entitled to.

Do you think you may be eligible for an age pension in time?

Are there any steps in this chapter (or the previous ones) that you can do to structure your assets so you may be entitled to more age pension in the future?

Deeming on my current superannuation balance (plus that of my partner, if I have one) is $_____

This means I would currently qualify for _____ (health care card).

Do you expect a material increase in your superannuation balance?

Will that mean your health care card entitlements change? How? _____

CHAPTER 10
Inheritance and the great wealth transfer

We are at the very beginning of the largest intergenerational wealth transfer in history, as generally wealthy baby boomers pass away and the next generation inherits their assets. It's estimated that by 2050, $3.5 trillion in assets will have changed hands within Australia, and it's highly likely you are unprepared for it.

Whether you're the baby boomer who will leave the inheritance or the Gen X or Gen Y on the receiving end, there are some things you need to know that will help you prepare for what's to come.

The addition of some level of inheritance makes all the difference for many of the clients I work with, and it's often the difference between having the financial resources to really retire life ready and living a more modest retirement than they were hoping for. The size of inheritances is increasing also.

With average home values sitting around $1 million or more, even just inheriting a house (perhaps even split with siblings) is a lot of money. If you could be on the receiving end of that, I want you to be well prepared to deal with it and also have given some thought to what you might do with it.

Talk about it

Both generations need to be having conversations about the wealth transfer, and the earlier the better. Open conversations about what you've got, what your assets are, where they are, how to access them and where your financial records are stored can reduce misunderstandings, ensure everyone's wishes are clearly communicated and make the whole process a lot smoother. Remember, it's going to be an incredibly emotional time dealing with the death of a loved one. Having conversations about all of this while all parties are still alive and without the emotion will make things easier for everyone.

If you have older parents, having them create a document with all their key information can be really helpful in the event that something happens to them. It's going to be much easier if you can easily find who you need to notify and are able to locate key documents. Use this list to help you get started:

- name and contact details of their primary care provider or other specialists

- medical conditions

- medications

- bank account details

- investment details

- super fund details

- insurance policy details

- pension details

- location of will

- power of attorney details

- emergency contacts

- funeral wishes

- passwords to computers or online accounts (be ultra careful how these are stored).

Revisit this list at least annually to ensure it remains up to date and add anything extra you think important to your particular relationship. This is a great tool for getting the conversation started about inheritance, the transfer of wealth and your (or your loved one's) wishes.

Get a will

It's estimated that 60 per cent of adult Australian's have a will. The number increases with age, with 88 per cent of people over 65 with a will and 93 per cent of people over the age of 70 with a will. With numbers that high for the over 65s, there must be a whole lot of 30 and 40 somethings who don't have one. It also means that 64 per cent of Australians with children under the age of 18 don't have a will.

Get a will.

You can get a will from a variety of different locations. My preference would be for you to visit a lawyer, and most suburban law firms deal with wills and estates. If you use a lawyer, they can help you ensure your will is correctly written, signed and witnessed, and they can advise on any complex situations — show me a family that doesn't have any complex situations!

Most states have a public trustee service that can prepare wills and also act as the executor of your will upon your death. They will charge your estate a fee for providing the executor service. You'll be able to find that service online for the state you live in.

Then, finally, you could get a will kit or use an online will platform. Will kits are available from newsagents and post offices, but you need to be incredibly careful that you complete the will kit correctly, sign appropriately and have it witnessed. Any estate planning lawyer I have ever spoken to says *do not* get a will kit, so proceed at your own risk (I wouldn't risk it).

A will deals with the distribution of your *estate* (this word is important and I'll come back to it shortly) upon your passing. If you die without a will, the state in which you live will follow what can be described as a formula for the distribution of your assets to your relatives. Dying without a will is called *dying intestate,* and each of the states and territories in Australia have different laws that determine who gets your assets and how much they get. So, if you don't want your state government deciding where your money goes, get a will.

Client story: Looking after your assets

Let's call this client Mary. Mary was an older lady who had been a client of ours for many, many years. We had helped Mary navigate retirement successfully, and in the last couple of years, she had moved into residential aged care. We assisted with that move and the financial impacts that came with it.

Mary was settled into aged care and, in more recent years, we had engaged Mary through her son Joe who held power of attorney for Mary. Everything was fine, and Mary's finances where ticking along. She had a small amount of savings and her age pension to pay for her aged care accommodation.

Mary also had a daughter (Joe's sister). The daughter was single, never married, no kids, and it was her intention to leave her assets to Joe's children since she had none of her own. Somewhat suddenly, the daughter died without a will. With no partner, no children and no will, the law in the state where the daughter lived said the next person in line to receive her assets were her parents, if they were still alive. So Mary inherited her daughter's assets, which included a life insurance benefit inside the daughter's superannuation fund.

After inheriting assets from her daughter, Mary lost her age pension. The means testing part of the aged care fees was recalculated, and Mary went to the maximum means tested care fee. If Mary gave the inherited assets to Joe's kids, like the daughter had wanted, the gifting rules would mean Mary couldn't get an age pension for five years.

The daughter's assets were now Mary's and would be distributed in accordance with Mary's will, but Mary no longer had the capacity to update her will. The spiderweb of a mess this all caused was incredible, all because the daughter hadn't made a will nominating her niece and nephew as beneficiaries.

Types of wills

There are two main types of wills: a basic will and a testamentary trust will.

With a basic will, you'll leave your assets to whoever you choose. They (the beneficiary) will receive those assets directly, and then do with them as they please. If those assets generate an income, the income will be added to the beneficiary's tax return and they will be taxed on those earnings, just the same as any other asset.

With a testamentary trust will, the beneficiary will typically have the option (i.e. they may not be forced) to take the assets they receive into a testamentary trust. A testamentary trust is a trust that comes into existence after the passing of the will maker, and if the beneficiary elects to receive their inheritance that way. Once the assets are inherited into the testamentary trust, the trust behaves much the same as any other trust.

As I described in Chapter 6, any income earned inside of a trust needs to be paid out to beneficiaries for the beneficiary to pay tax. A testamentary trust (versus a basic will) has the advantage of being able to distribute the income to different people for the best tax treatment, this includes children under the age of 18. If a child under the age of 18 receives income from a testamentary trust, they are taxed on that income as an adult. This means the child has the benefit of the tax-free threshold and all the normal marginal tax rates. A child ordinarily can't take advantage of these thresholds if they earn 'unearned income' in their own name. Income from a testamentary trust is an exception to this.

The other major benefit of a testamentary trust is asset protection. Between a couple, you might use a testamentary trust to keep your assets for the benefit of your children, lessening the likelihood that the survivor's new partner runs off with some of the money. It can help keep assets in your family and provide a degree of protection from external creditors or anyone else who might come after your beneficiary for some money.

Have a chat with your lawyer about the pros and cons of each will type and get some legal advice.

Estate assets

Your will can only deal with some of the assets you own, the ones that are covered under *estate assets*. Some examples of estate assets are:

- bank accounts held in the name of the deceased only

- shares held in the name of the deceased only

- life insurance policies where the deceased nominated their estate as the beneficiary

- property either owned individually or as a tenant in common with someone else

- personal belongings

- pets.

Non-estate assets on the other hand are assets not included in a person's estate and, therefore, not controlled by their will, some examples are:

- jointly owned assets

- superannuation

- assets in a trust

- assets in a company.

Jointly owned assets

Jointly owned assets, such as bank accounts, shares or property, are automatically inherited by the deceased's joint owner. The registered owner of the asset will need to be updated to reflect the new ownership by the joint owner or owners.

Assets owned as *tenant in common* with the deceased are treated differently to jointly owned assets. When you own an asset as a tenant in common, you have an individually identifiable ownership of a percentage of the asset — you might own 50 per cent, you might own 5 per cent or any other percentage. When a tenant in common dies, the other owner (or owners) don't automatically take over ownership. The deceased's share is left via their will (or intestacy laws if they don't have a will) to a beneficiary, that may be the other owners of the asset or it could be someone entirely different.

Superannuation

The distribution of your superannuation benefits to beneficiaries isn't covered by your will in the first instance. The distribution of your superannuation is covered by your beneficiary nomination on your superannuation account. There are two ways that your superannuation fund will pay benefits to your estate. These are if you:

1. have nominated your *estate* as the beneficiary of your superannuation

2. don't have a valid superannuation beneficiary nomination, in which case your fund may decide to pay benefits to your estate.

When it comes to beneficiaries of your superannuation fund, there are only a very small number of people you may be able to leave your superannuation to directly (outside of your will), they are:

- your spouse (including de facto)

- your child

- a person you have an interdependency relationship with.

Often, your superannuation fund will accept a beneficiary nomination form with your parent, sibling or your niece or nephew on it (all of whom you generally can't nominate unless you have an interdependency relationship with them). Just because they haven't rejected your form doesn't mean they will pay your superannuation to that person. It's only upon your death that your relationship with the nominated beneficiary will be tested by your superannuation fund, and if you have an invalid beneficiary nominated, then the superannuation fund's trustee will decide where to pay your superannuation for you (after taking into account your relationship with various people in your life).

If you want to leave your superannuation to anyone who isn't your spouse, child or someone you have an interdependency relationship with, then you might need to nominate your estate and have your will take care of the distribution of money. Work with the lawyer you have draft your will to ensure you've got your superannuation beneficiary nominated correctly.

There are several ways of nominating a beneficiary on your superannuation fund, these include:

- **Binding nomination:** With this type of nomination, the trustee of your superannuation fund is bound to pay your superannuation to whom you nominate (provided the person you have nominated is on the allowable list).

If the person you have nominated isn't on the eligible list, or you haven't completed your binding nomination form correctly, the nomination becomes invalid and you're back to the trustee deciding where your money goes.

■ **Non-binding nomination:** With this type of nomination, you are instructing the trustee of your superannuation fund (the people who control your superannuation fund) of whom you wish them to consider paying your benefits to. They are not bound to follow a non-binding nomination, and for various reasons, they may decide to pay your super to someone else or to your estate.

■ **Reversionary beneficiary:** This type of nomination is relevant for pension accounts. It doesn't matter if you have a defined benefit pension or an ordinary account-based (accumulation) pension, the idea here is broadly the same. When you appoint a reversionary beneficiary, the beneficiary takes over your pension fund after your death, and has the pension payments made to them. With a defined benefit fund, ordinarily, some fraction of what you received gets paid to your reversionary spouse, maybe 67 per cent. With an account-based (accumulation) style pension the beneficiary takes over whatever your account balance is. It's mostly only your spouse who can be the reversionary beneficiary; outside of that it's near impossible to pay a reversionary pension to anyone else.

Assets in a trust or company

If you own assets in a trust or a company, you don't directly own the assets and, therefore, can't leave them to someone in your will. In the case of a company, you might own the shares in a private company that, in turn, owns some assets (maybe a business, stock market–listed shares, property or some other asset). You can leave the shares in the private company you own to someone in your will, but you cannot directly will the assets of the company to someone.

The same idea applies to assets held in a trust. You don't own the assets held in a trust. You might control the trust and be able to direct the investments of the trust, but you don't own the assets, and, as such, you can't will them to someone. In your will, you can leave the positions of trustee and appointer to someone who, in turn, takes over control of the trust and can then make decisions about the assets and running of the trust (see figure 10.1).

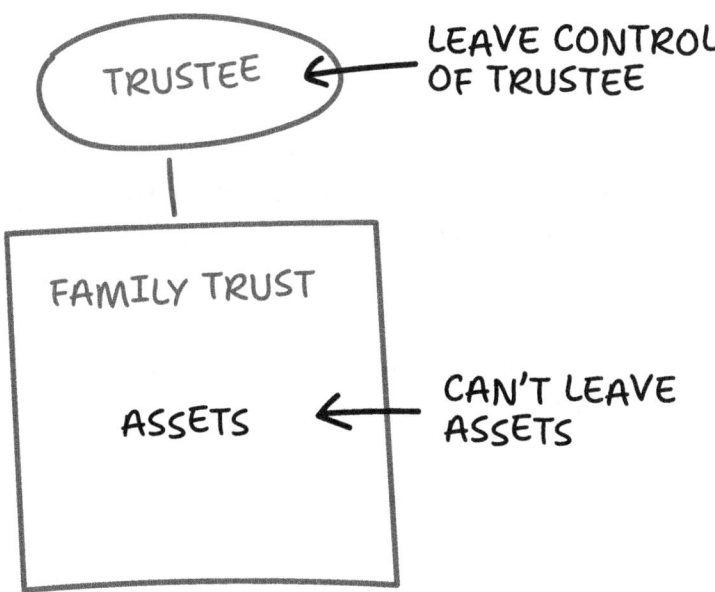

Figure 10.1: Family trust: Who controls what

Power of attorney

A power of attorney is a legal document that lets someone else make decisions on your behalf. It allows the attorney to conduct financial, legal or personal affairs for you. Importantly, the power of attorney only operates when the principal (the person granting the authority to another) is alive; when the principal dies, the attorney ceases to have any power.

If you have older parents, it's incredibly important you ensure they have granted a power of attorney to someone, ideally someone younger than them (perhaps you). It's very common for partners to grant power of attorney to each other, but if they are both older, you can find yourself in a situation where the attorney doesn't really have the capacity to make decisions themselves, so holding power of attorney for someone else is kind of useless.

For yourself as well, when you have your will drawn up by a lawyer, please take up their offer of preparing power of attorney documents for you too. It can be convenient for someone to act on your behalf if you are unable to, perhaps you're away for work or, worse, some accident leaves you incapable of making decisions for yourself. Without a power of attorney document, your family will need to apply to the courts to be granted the power, which is a headache that is easily avoided by just having a power of attorney in the first place.

Tax on inheritance

We don't have an inheritance tax in Australia, like those that exist in some other countries. Aside from superannuation (discussed in Chapter 7), you do not have to pay any tax just because you've inherited something from someone else. But that's not to say there won't possibly be some tax consequences for you depending on what you inherit and what you do with that inheritance.

As I said at the beginning of this chapter, it's estimated that $3.5 trillion will change hands in Australia by 2050. For most people, that's likely to be made up of some combination of the following four types of assets:

1. cash

2. primary residence

3. superannuation

4. shares and investment properties.

I'll explore the things you need to know about inheriting each of these assets in the sections that follow.

1. Inheriting cash

Cash is inherited entirely tax free. Cash isn't subject to capital gains tax, so you don't have any of those complications to deal with. You just deposit it into your account and do with it as you please.

Obviously, if you start to earn interest on the cash or choose to invest it, any earnings will then be subject to tax. The earnings get added on top of any other income you earn in a financial year, and you are taxed according to the ordinary marginal tax rates.

2. Inheriting a primary residence

With any type of property you may inherit, it's important you have details and records of how that property was used. If a property was used as an investment or holiday home before becoming someone's primary residence, for example, there will be different tax consequences than if the home was just used as a primary residence the whole time it was owned by the deceased.

If you inherit a deceased person's home and that property was only ever used as the deceased's primary residence, you are granted a two-year window from the date of death to dispose of the property without incurring any capital gains tax liability. This is to recognise that the deceased could have sold the property themselves while they were alive, and they wouldn't have had to pay capital gains tax. So, if you sell it soon after their death (within two years), you won't have to pay any capital gains tax either.

If, however, you decide to keep the property, but you don't move into it and make it your primary residence, it will be subject to capital gains tax just like any other investment property or holiday home. The value of the property at the date of the deceased's death becomes the cost base and any increase in value from there to when you eventually sell (assuming you sell more than two years after death) becomes a gain that the ordinary capital gains tax calculation applies to.

Alternatively, you may inherit someone's home and choose to live in it as your primary residence yourself. If that's the case, the home will continue to be exempt from capital gains tax as long as you treat it as your primary residence.

3. Inheriting superannuation

Superannuation benefits are made up of two components: the taxable component and the tax-free component. What makes up each component is determined by how the money got into the superannuation fund in the first place, and the types of contributions made into your superannuation fund.

I discussed superannuation in detail in Chapter 7. You might remember this diagram showing concessional contributions, which add to the taxable component of your superannuation balance. The non-concessional or downsizer contributions add to the tax-free component of your superannuation balance (see figure 10.2).

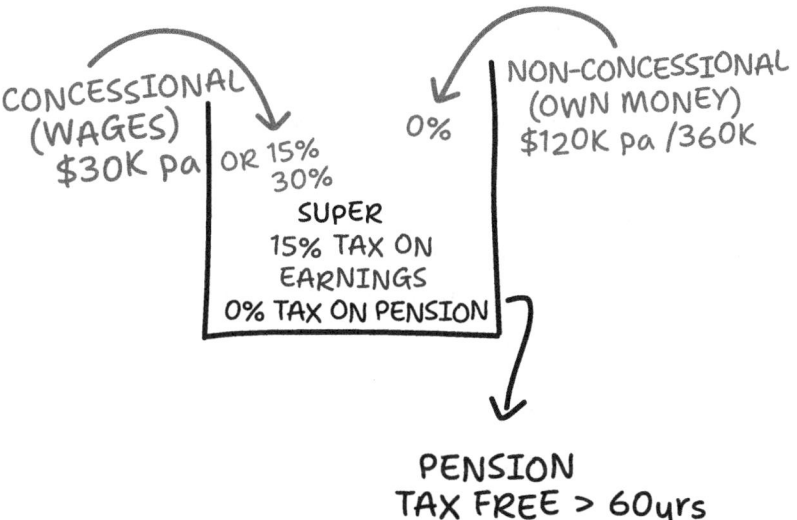

Figure 10.2: The superannuation bucket: How concessional and non-concessional contributions flow in

If superannuation is inherited by one of the following people, they will inherit the full balance tax free:

■ spouse, including de facto partner

■ former spouse

- child under 18

- person in an interdependency relationship.

There's one big group of superannuation beneficiaries who *don't* make the list — your children over the age of 18.

If superannuation is inherited by anyone who isn't on that list, it's likely they will have to pay tax. If we're talking about the great wealth transfer, it's most commonly going to be baby boomer parents leaving assets to their adult children, in which case, inherited superannuation will likely come with some tax to pay.

If you're not on the list and you do inherit some superannuation, you will have to pay some tax on the taxable component (the concessional contributions + investment earnings), which is a maximum of 15 per cent + Medicare (total of 17 per cent) if you receive the money directly from the superannuation fund, or taxed at 15 per cent (without Medicare) if you receive it from the deceased's estate (that is the money is paid from the super fund to the deceased's estate, then their will distributes the money to you).

There is something that can be done to help reduce or eliminate this tax but you're going to want to seek some financial advice. There's a strategy we implement for most of our retired clients where we have them take a lump sum withdrawal from their superannuation fund (tax free) then contribute that same money back into superannuation using the non-concessional contribution cap. If you have enough time, it's possible to eventually withdraw all of your superannuation balance and re-contribute it as non-concessional contributions. This makes the whole balance a tax-free component, and then, regardless of who inherits the super or how they inherit it, the superannuation will be inherited tax free (see figure 10.3). Please seek some professional advice about this strategy.

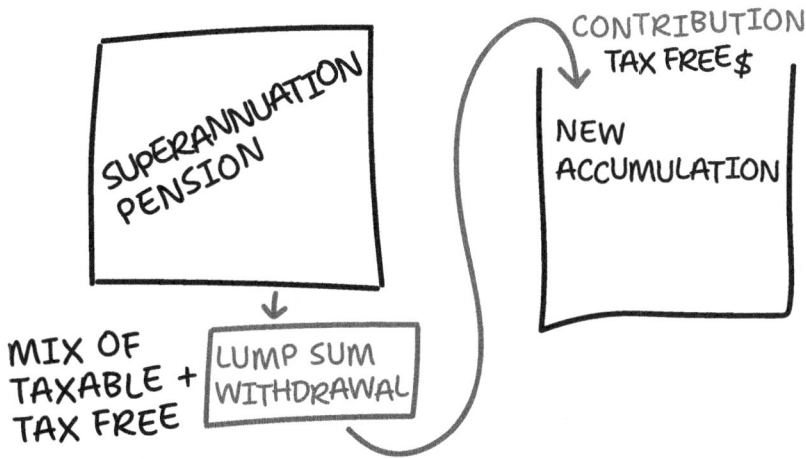

Figure 10.3: The recontribution strategy: How to turn taxable super into a tax-free inheritance

4. Inheriting shares or investment property

Inheriting shares and investment properties have similar implications so I'll tackle them together. As I've said before, the act of you inheriting either shares or an investment property doesn't trigger any tax; however, if you decide to sell what you've inherited, you may need to pay capital gains tax.

Firstly, you're going to need to know when the deceased purchased the asset that you are inheriting. If they purchased it before September 1985, then the asset will be called a pre-capitals gains tax asset. This means that if you sell the asset shortly after the date of death, you'll be able to do so without any capital gains tax implications.

If you decide to keep the pre-capitals gains tax asset, it becomes a post-capitals gains tax asset on the date of death, and any increase in value from the date of death to when you decide to sell will be subject to the ordinary capital gains tax calculation.

Now if the deceased purchased the asset after September 1985, capital gains tax is applicable and you'll pay the tax if you choose to sell and you sell at a price higher than the asset was originally purchased for. When you inherit an asset that was purchased after September 1985, you also inherit the cost base of the asset, that is you inherit the original purchase price and any changes that may have occurred along the way to adjust the cost base.

Let me explain with an example. Let's say your parents purchased some shares in CSL when they first listed on the stock market in 1994, the price of which was $0.76 when you adjust for stock splits. Now, suppose you inherit those CSL shares from your parents and you decide to sell those shares. In January 2025, you could have sold a CSL share for around $285. The gain in the share price from 1994 through to January 2025 becomes assessable to you using the ordinary capital gains tax calculation explained on page 111. I see CSL and CBA inheritances very regularly in my work. The inheritance is making the next generation very wealthy, but it also comes with a very big tax headache that needs to be managed.

If you don't sell the inherited asset, no capital gains tax is payable. Eventually, the asset will then be inherited by someone else and the capital gains tax 'problem' becomes theirs. The liability for capital gains tax never goes away, it just keeps being passed down from one person to the next.

Inheritance and Services Australia

One of the, sometimes unexpected, side effects of an inheritance is the impact on a beneficiary's Services Australia entitlements. If you inherit some money or other assets, it's obviously going to increase your own asset position. If you are in receipt of some form of benefit from Services Australia, perhaps the age pension or one of the health care cards I mentioned in Chapter 9, then your increased asset position may mean you lose that benefit, just like my client Joe from page 186 did.

I'm contacted multiple times a year by people who have either already inherited or are about to inherit while they are in receipt of the age pension. Lots of people who are on the age pension don't really want to disrupt what they have going on, they would often rather see the money they are about to inherit go to their own children — skipping a generation.

The problem is, if you try to give away an inheritance you receive (or any other assets for that matter) and you are in receipt of some form of Services Australia benefit, you will be caught under the gifting rules. Your asset position will increase as a result of the inheritance, and Services Australia will either reduce or even cut off your age pension (if you inherit enough) as a result of the inheritance. If you then decide to give away the inheritance, Services Australia will count anything in excess of $10000 you give away as an asset of yours even though you don't have the money anymore, meaning your age pension entitlements will still be reduced.

Services Australia's gifting rules allow you to gift $10000 per financial year and a maximum of $30000 over a five-year period. Anything in excess of this will count as your asset (even though you no longer have it) for five years from the date of the gift.

This is a great example of where an open conversation about what you have and what someone may inherit could be really beneficial. If you're able to, you could have a conversation with the will maker and explain your position. Perhaps you could ask them to leave any inheritance that may have otherwise been paid to you to your children. It gives the grandkids a nice head start, and may save you a whole lot of headache when it comes to lost benefits. Think about this as you get older and how you might leave your own inheritance.

Gifting assets while you're still alive

Where you have the means to, gifting assets to your beneficiaries while you are still alive can be very rewarding for you. A financial advice colleague of mine put it like this:

Often retirees wait until they pass to share their wealth with their adult children, by which time, those adult children have all grown up and their mortgages are paid off.

The money you gift your adult children while you're still alive is most helpful to them because they are going through the most capital-intensive period of their lives with mortgages, often raising young children and education funding. Your gift can ease a lot of their financial stress during this period.

This is becoming increasingly common for parents who want to give their children some form of financial assistance early on in their adult lives. I speak with parents on a daily basis who want to save up and invest some money so that they can help their children buy their first home. Sometimes inheritance plays a role here. It's encouraging to see just how many people comment something along the lines of, 'We want to do what we can within our own means to support our own retirement, so that any inheritance we do receive can be used to help our kids'. As horrible as it is to say, it's not a great retirement plan to wait for someone to die so you can inherit, and then yourself be in a position to retire.

Much like the announcement as the airplane is about to take off that says 'fit your own mask first before helping others', the same applies with your finances. The goal of helping your child buy their first home is amazing, and what a feeling it must be to achieve that, but you must first make sure your finances are robust enough to support yourself before you go giving away lump sums of money. One of the worst things you can do for your child is help them buy a home, only to turn around and have them need to support you in retirement, pay their own mortgage, run their own household and support you too. Fit your own mask first.

If you are going to go down the route of gifting some of your assets while you are still alive, there are a couple of major differences from what I've described earlier in this chapter when I was discussing inheritance:

- Transfers of property while you are still alive are subject to stamp duty. That same transfer as part of a deceased estate is not subject to stamp duty.

- Capital gains becomes payable by the person gifting the asset. Even though you might give away the asset for free, it is still deemed as a disposal at market value for the purposes of capital gains tax. If the asset you are gifting is worth more when you gift it than what it was when you purchased it, the transfer will be subject to capital gains tax. As I discussed earlier, inheriting an asset doesn't trigger capital gains tax — tax is only payable if you decide to sell the asset after inheriting it and gifting an asset while you are alive is considered a sale.

■ Be aware of the Services Australia gifting rules.
I discussed these on page 201, but if you are going to give away assets, the value of that asset (if above gifting limits) will count as yours for five years, even though you no longer have the asset. If you gift your home, an asset that is exempt from Services Australia assessment, as soon as you gift it, the value of the home will count as an asset and any Services Australia benefits you may receive will be adjusted according to the new total asset figure you have.

Inheriting debts

While there will be a vast amount of wealth changing hands over the coming years, so will a lot of debt. When you die, your debts don't disappear. Upon your death, student debt (HECS/HELP) is wiped by the government and usually your bank will wipe any debt you've accrued on a credit card. Outside of that, whoever inherits your assets will also inherit your debt.

In the time that I've been writing this book, I've had four phone calls from people looking for assistance after inheriting a property from their parents that came with a reverse mortgage. A reverse mortgage is where the owner has taken a loan from a bank, secured against their home, where the money from the loan is used to help fund living needs. That loan is usually repaid when the property is sold. However, if the person who inherits the home intends to keep the house, they have to find another way to pay off the loan. Prior to these four phone calls, I hadn't had one in all the years I've been working in financial advice. I suspect that, over the coming years, this will become more of a regular occurrence.

All four people planned to keep the properties they had inherited, either to move into as their own homes or keep as investment properties. All four will need to speak with a mortgage broker to arrange an ordinary bank loan to pay out the reverse mortgage so that they can keep the houses.

If you're likely to leave someone a debt, or you are likely to inherit one, it's all the more reason to have the conversation up front so that everyone can be prepared.

Get your house in order

In making sure your house is in order for when the inevitable occurs, make sure you have a will and make sure your parents have a will. If your parents are older, perhaps encouraging them to appoint someone other than their spouse as a power of attorney may be a good idea.

Make sure you have valid and up-to-date beneficiary nomination on your superannuation fund, make sure your parents have valid nominations on theirs too. Remember it's not just the super balance that may be paid to someone, it's your life insurance benefits too. This could very easily be a very big number.

Understand the tax implications of keeping/selling inherited assets. Inheritance can either be the icing on the cake to you hitting your net nest egg asset number and retiring life ready or it could be used to skip a generation and give your children a head start.

Retire life ready steps

While ensuring your estate planning is in order can be as simple as making sure you have an appropriate will in place, as you can see from this chapter, there's actually a lot more than that to think about.

Refer back to the table of assets you created in Chapter 2. Are these estate assets that can be dealt with via your will, such as individual bank accounts, real estate and stocks?

For those assets that aren't estate assets, do you have appropriate things in place (such as superannuation beneficiary nominations) that will direct those assets to the right place?

Is it time to have a meaningful conversation with your parents, and perhaps make a list like the one on page 184? Perhaps it's a good time to talk to them about their own estate planning wishes to make sure those plans are in place while they can still do something about it.

As with a number of sections through this book, to execute the actions in this chapter properly you will need the assistance of professionals, namely an estate planning lawyer for this chapter.

CHAPTER 11

Helping your loved ones navigate aged care

I feel it important to include a chapter on aged care in this book, not because you will need it any time soon, but because you will probably be the person helping your parents navigate the system. They need someone to advocate for them, and in order for you to do that, you need to have an understanding of the system.

This is a highly emotional time for a family. Watching a loved one's health decline to such an extent that they can no longer, safely, remain in their own home is hard. It's common to feel guilty about not being able to be there and provide the help they need. Then, all of a sudden, your family is thrust into the world of aged care, and having to deal with My Aged Care, Services

Australia, care providers, aged care homes and then all the numbers start — it is a very difficult time for most families.

I'm convinced the fees for residential aged care, which I will discuss further in this chapter, put the most strain on a retiree's finances, far more than any other stage of their retirement. It's even more of a strain if they are part of a couple, where one person needs to move into residential aged care while the other continues to live in the home.

Through this chapter, I hope to give you a solid understanding of how the system works and where all the different fees come into play for if and when the time comes that a family member needs increased levels of care. Even if it's to know that you need to seek specialist financial advice, my hope is that it won't all be completely foreign to you.

My Aged Care and ACAT/ACAS

The aged care system starts with the My Aged Care website and your Aged Care Assessment Team (ACAT) and Aged Care Assessment Service (ACAS) assessment. Before you can get anywhere with the federal aged care system, visit myagedcare.gov.au and organise an ACAT/ACAS assessment.

We encourage people to register in the system before they think they will need assistance. It can take months for an ACAT/ACAS assessment to be completed (unless it's being done while the person is in hospital), so it's best to do this when you aren't in a whole lot of rush for it.

I've also found that people who think they don't need any help at home, and are otherwise living well independently, sometimes qualify for a low-level home care package. Take the assistance if you qualify for it and use it for something that will make your life easier — that's what it's there for.

The results of the assessment will be a determination of the level of assistance your loved one qualifies for. It could be nothing, it could be some form of home care package or it could be residential aged care.

Support at Home

The federal aged care system starts with Support at Home packages, which are assigned a level from 1 (which comes with a low level of assistance) to 8 (which comes with more financial assistance) for ongoing support PLUS 2 additional short term packages.

Support at Home packages are, as the name suggests, Federal Government packages designed to provide you assistance in your own home. To allow you to stay in your home for as long as possible. The contribution you make together with the Government's contribution give you an 'allowance' you can spend on a wide range of services to the home. Cleaning, gardening, washing... the list is extensive.

After you've completed the physical and mental assessments to determine whether you qualify or not, an assessment is also done of your financial means and, depending on the outcome of that assessment, you may be required to contribute an amount towards your Support at Home package. The government will then top up your contribution with an extra allowance that you can then spend on a menu of available services from your selected care provider.

At level 1, you'll have an annual budget of around $11 000 to spend on services, whilst at level 8 you'll have around $78 000. How much the individual may have to contribute towards their Support at Home annual budget will depend on their financial circumstances and what they are spending the package on, as follows:

Type of service	Full Pensioner	Part Pensioner	Self-funded retiree
Clinical support	0%	0%	0%
Independence services	5%	5–50%	50%
Everyday living services	17.5%	17.5–80%	80%

Source: © Commonwealth of Australia.

Residential aged care

If your care needs go beyond being able to stay in your own home, then residential aged care is the next step. Like with the home care packages, you first need to have the ACAT/ACAS assessment done, and be assessed as needing residential aged care. Without such an assessment, you cannot enter residential aged care.

Next, you need to find a facility you like that also has room to accommodate you. Sometimes facilities have waiting lists, and other times they have empty rooms. If the facility has multiple empty rooms, you're a chance at being able to negotiate a cheaper price for the room. I've managed to negotiate cheaper room prices for a few clients. If you don't ask, you'll never know.

My top tip for finding an appropriate facility is to make sure it's close by (to you, not necessarily close by to where your parents currently live) so you can visit often and advocate for your loved one going into care. If it's your mum or dad going into care, there's not a lot of point having them go into a facility that is near where they currently live if you're the person who's going to be vising them most often and checking on them and you live nowhere near there. Find a facility you and your mum or dad will be comfortable with, but please make sure it's close enough to you that you can visit often.

Some of my clients whose partners have gone into care, go and visit morning and night. The facilities are walking distance away from where they live, so getting there and back home again is a breeze.

Residential aged care finances

I said back on page 208 that I'm convinced residential aged care, where one member of a couple needs care and the other is still capable of living at home, is the biggest financial challenge retirees face.

The cost of residential aged care is broken up into three parts, and we're going to look at each one in detail (see figure 11.1, overleaf). The three parts are:

1. room

2. care

3. additional services.

Figure 11.1: Breaking down aged care costs: How room, care and extras add up in retirement

1. ROOM

The easiest way to think about the cost of a room is that you either 'buy' the right to occupy the room by paying the advertised rate up front or you 'rent' the room by paying a prescribed interest rate multiplied by the cost of the room. That interest rate is fixed at the time you become a permanent resident and will only change if you leave the aged care facility and enter another one.

For example, a room may cost $600 000. If you have the means, you could pay the $600 000 upfront. Alternatively, you could pay the interest rate of 8.17 per cent (current at June 2025) on $600 000, which is $49 020 per annum (often charged in monthly instalments).

You can also do combination of both, so part 'buy' the room and part 'rent' the room.

If you elect to pay the full cost of the room, the facility will deduct 2 per cent every year of the room cost from the lump sum payment you have made for a maximum of five years. So if you reside in care for long enough, upon leaving (either voluntarily or as a result of death), only 90 per cent of the fee you paid for the room will be returned to you/your estate. The facility keeps the other 10 per cent.

If you elect to pay the cost of the room via interest payment, the interest rate, as I mentioned, is fixed. However, the cost of the room that the interest rate is multiplied by will be indexed up each year, which means your interest bill will increase every year.

Figuring out how to pay for the cost of a room (Do you pay the full cost upfront? Do you pay interest or some combination of both?), then where the money comes from to pay for either choice is a specialist area of financial advice. I can't emphasise enough how stressful this situation can be for you if you are navigating it on your own — please get some help from a financial adviser.

2. CARE

The cost of your care is broken up into two parts, the first being the basic daily fee that every resident pays, which is set at 85 per cent of the full rate of the single age pension and increases every six months in line with increases to the age pension. As at March 2025, the basic daily fee was $63.57 per day or the equivalent of $23 203.05 per annum. Even aged care residents with very little in the way of assets will still have the means to pay this fee as the resident will be in receipt of a full age pension (current rates of the pension can be found on page 165).

The second part of your care cost, known as the Hoteling Supplement Contribution (HSC) is means tested — the more financial means you have, the more you will be asked to contribute to the cost of your own care (with less funded by the Government). There are two different parts to the means testing but all you really need to know is that the more assets you have or the more income you have, the more you will be asked to pay up to a daily limit of $12.55 per day.

The final part of your care cost, known as the non-clinical care contribution (NCCC), replaces what was the means tested care fee. Like the Hoteling Supplement Contribution it is also means tested based on the residents income and assets up to a daily limit of $101.16. There are lifetime caps on non-clinical care contribution at a lifetime limit of $130 000 (indexed) or four years in care. If the resident meets either one of these limits, their means testing fee will stop.

How you choose to structure the payment of the room cost will have an impact on the result of your means testing — all the more reason to get advice.

3. ADDITIONAL SERVICES

Over and above the basics of residing in care, you can choose to take up some of the additional services the facility may offer. This might be things like wine with dinner, Foxtel or Netflix, or some other benefits the facility offers.

These services cannot be a condition of entry (as they often were in the past). The agreement must outline the cost of each higher service to be delivered, the standard, frequency and how they will be charged. Residents cannot be asked to pay for a service they cannot use. A 28 day cooling off period applies and after the 28 days, the service can be cancelled by the resident with 28 days notice.

Do you have the means?

The fee structure I've just described for residential aged care is for those who are assessed as having the means to pay. Some people enter aged care with what's called *low means*. Their assets are at such a level that following a Services Australia assessment, they determine the resident cannot afford the advertised price for a room in the aged care facility.

If that is the case, a separate calculation is done based on the assets the resident does have to determine the amount of money the resident can afford to pay. This amount can then be paid as an ongoing daily amount (think more like the rent description on page 212) or converted to a lump sum and paid in one hit.

If the resident's assets (or their half share of combined assets with their partner) are below $61 500, they won't have to pay anything towards the cost of the room. If the resident's assets (or their half share of combined assets with their partner) are above $61 500 but below $206 039.20, they will have to contribute something towards the cost of the room, based on a calculation of what they can afford to pay. Then, if the resident's assets (or their half share of combined assets with their partner) are above $206 039.20, they will have to pay the advertised price for the room.

Client story: Navigating the means assessment

A few years back, one of my long-term clients needed to enter residential aged care, while their partner stayed living in the home. We had done our own assessment of their financial position and concluded that the person going into care would be assessed as low means, so they would pay a reduced accommodation charge, rather than the advertised price for a room. Even at the lower room charge, things were going to be tight. They already received the full age pension, so the family agreed they would also contribute towards the annual care costs.

(continued)

After all the paperwork was lodged, the assessment came back from Services Australia stating that the resident had means to pay the full room cost. *How?* They absolutely didn't have the means and, if they did have to pay the full room cost, they would run out of money completely within three years. Turns out there were some issues with how Services Australia was assessing a family trust this couple once operated. The trust was still in existence but hadn't really been used for many years. Tax returns were well behind and Services Australia had issue with how some of the past operations of the trust had been accounted for.

They were getting letters from Services Australia asking for more and more information, while the aged care home was demanding payment for the room. It was a hugely stressful position for the family to be in. Fortunately, we had been involved from the beginning so we were able to support the family through it, but it took two years of reporting to Services Australia and waiting on their assessments to get the correct means assessment back. There's no way they could have done it on their own.

Does the home count?

The value of the home the aged care resident leaves to then move into aged care counts as an asset in some circumstances and doesn't in others.

If the person moving into care is single, and no-one else was living in the home at the time they move into care, then the home will be counted as an asset for aged care means testing at a capped value of $206 039.20. This means any single person who owns a home will be assessed as having the means to pay the advertised price for a room in aged care. Often the home gets sold to pay for the room in aged care.

Alternatively, if someone who meets the definition of a protected person (see the list following) resides in the home with the person who moves into aged care, the value of the home is completely ignored for aged care means testing assessment. Given the home doesn't count as an asset in this case, it's somewhat common for the first member of a couple, for example, to move into aged care and be assessed as having low means. If the second member of the couple later needs to move into aged care, the second person will be assessed as having means because the capped value of the house counts as an asset.

A protected person is one of the following:

- your partner or your dependent child

- a carer who has lived with you for at least two years and is eligible for income support

- a close relation, such as a sister, brother, parent, child or grandchild, who has lived with you for the past five years and is eligible for income support.

Notice the reference to income support. It's not enough to have carer or a sibling, for example, living with you. That person also needs to be eligible for income support. They don't have to be a recipient of income support, but they do have to be eligible for it.

The protected person exemption is lost as soon as the protected person moves out of the home or if they no longer qualify for an income support payment.

Age pension and your home

The final complication with residential aged care is how the age pension interacts with your decision to keep or sell the home after someone moves into aged care. If a protected person resides in the home, and they remain a protected person, the value of the home will continue to be exempt for aged care means testing. However, Services Australia assesses the home differently for age pension purposes.

For the age pension, a former home will generally be exempt from age pension assessment for two years after the individual enters aged care. After two years, Services Australia will assess the full value of the house (unless your partner continues to reside in the home), which typically means the aged care resident will have their age pension cut significantly or cancelled completely.

This two-year window exists to give the resident and family some time to sort out what they are doing with the house. Given losing the age pension can have a big impact on someone's cash flow, you'll often have a particular way of managing the aged care costs for the first couple of years, then have another way of managing the costs after the two years is up and/or you sell the house, whichever happens first.

If the house is sold, the proceeds received from selling the house become assessable for age pension purposes, and the full value counts for aged care means testing, and is not just capped at the value of $206039.20.

Check the limits

As with other topics in this book, you should check the various limits at the time you are assisting someone with the aged care system. Things like home care packages, basic daily fees and the capped value of your home all get increased over time.

Having the most up-to-date information at the time you need it (i.e. when you are trying to navigate the system), will ensure you can structure your finances to optimise your savings. Being aware of what might affect your full or part age pension lets you make informed choices that allow you to enjoy this period of life without financial worry.

As we've been working towards throughout the first two parts of this book, we want to retire life ready in a way that supports our ongoing health, wealth and happiness. In Part III, we're going to explore how you can put all this information to work and make sure you close the gap between where you are now and where you want to be when you retire.

Retire life ready steps

I suspect most people reading this book are likely to, at some point, assist their parents in navigating the aged care system.

As your parents age, encourage them to register for My Aged Care (myagedcare.gov.au) and have an assessment done. It is much easier for everyone involved if your parents are registered before something urgent happens. If residential aged care is necessary, more often than not, it's something that happens quickly after a trip to hospital. Do what you can now, well in advance of that rushed situation – it will be better for everyone.

Spend some time understanding how the aged care system works from a financial perspective so that it's not so overwhelming when you have to help a loved one through it.

Visit the My Aged Care website and plug in your parents financial details so you can have an idea of what the costs may be. Do not pay the refundable accommodation deposit (RAD) for your parents before getting some financial advice. We see lots of kids trying to be helpful and paying the RAD for Mum and Dad only to find it makes the situation worse.

Please get some help. This whole topic is highly emotional and can be financially stressful. Some expert help is worth its weight in gold here.

PART III
Closing the gap

You may be coming to this section of the book not feeling quite so confident about the financial position you are in, and your ability to close the gap on your ideal retirement. If this is you, the following chapters will hopefully give you some confidence around improving that situation, and even if you don't make it to 20x your ideal spending number, it's still possible to have an amazing retirement on less and get a top-up from the age pension. I've worked with plenty of clients over the years who will back me up on that.

We'll look at where your current trajectory is taking you as a baseline. Then, if that needs improving, we'll look at how the allocation of any surplus income you have can close the gap, before taking it a step further with some basic financial moves. We'll then finish by looking at how you manage the transition from accumulating assets to living off what you've built.

CHAPTER 12

Where are you headed?

In Chapter 2, you worked out where you are financially *now*. Looking at the assets you own, and the debts that you owe, you worked out a number we called your *net nest egg assets*. In Chapter 3, you worked out your ideal position to retire life ready. Before we get too stuck into the final section of this book, have a quick look back at those two numbers so they are fresh in your mind before we continue on.

In this chapter, the exercises will help you get an understanding of where your current financial trajectory is taking you so that you can identify if you're on track or if there are some adjustments you'll need to make to ensure that you can retire and live the best version of your life that you dreamed up in Chapter 1.

Keep things simple

My preference is to try and keep things as simple as possible when it comes to closing the gap. You can come up with all kinds of elaborate plans to build your wealth using property, debt, negative gearing, shares, super, trusts and companies — it can very quickly become so complicated that you lose sight of what you are actually trying to do.

In Australia, there are two key requirements to a comfortable retirement:

1. own your own home

2. have enough money in other assets to provide an income to support that retirement, with the backup of the age pension system.

Owning your own home isn't for everyone, but it is for most. The retirement system we have here in Australia works far more in your favour if you own the home you live in than if you don't. I can appreciate it is becoming increasingly more difficult to purchase a home in Australia, and even those who have managed to purchase are finding it more difficult to repay their mortgage and do everything else that is 'expected' for retirement.

The reason I say the Australian retirement system works far more in your favour if you own the home you live in is to do with the age pension and health care card system we covered in Chapter 8. You can have a far greater level of assets and still get some level of government support if you own your own home than if you don't. Add into the mix that your retirement expenses are less if you aren't paying rent, and you can appreciate why owning your own home is number one on the list.

Paying off your debts

The first element of working out where you are headed is to understand how long it will take you to pay off your debts, ideally, so that you own you own home by the time you get to retirement, and have some other assets to help support your retirement.

You'll recall from the net nest egg asset calculation you conducted in Chapter 2 that your debts get subtracted from your assets. So, one of the easiest things you can do to boost your net nest egg asset number is pay off your debts. We'll look at whether paying off your debts is the smartest use of your money later, but for now, let's look at how long it might take you.

For most households, their largest debt will be their mortgage, and if not on their own home, then perhaps debt on an investment property. If you remember, in calculating your net nest egg number, you don't include the value of your own home in the assets, but you do include the value of your outstanding mortgage as a liability.

You can use an online calculator (try the one on my website at jameswrigley.com.au) to help you work out how long it will take you to pay off your mortgage at your current interest rate and rate of repayment. The following table will help you estimate it.

This table has been prepared at a 6 per cent interest rate, which, in March 2025, is about the going rate of a mortgage. Locate the approximate outstanding balance of your home loan down the left column. If you have money sitting in your offset account, subtract that from your outstanding loan balance. Now move across the rows to the number that most closely aligns with the monthly repayments you are currently making. The row across the top will give you an indication of how long it will take you to repay your mortgage at that current repayment rate.

Remember these repayments are covering the principal of your loan as well as the interest bill, so working out what you need to repay is more complicated than dividing your outstanding loan balance by the number of years you want to repay it.

| Loan | Years | | | | | |
	5	10	15	20	25	30
$100 000	$1933	$1110	$844	$716	$644	$600
$150 000	$2900	$1665	$1266	$1075	$966	$899
$200 000	$3867	$2220	$1688	$1433	$1289	$1199
$250 000	$4833	$2776	$2110	$1791	$1611	$1499
$300 000	$5800	$3331	$2532	$2149	$1933	$1799
$350 000	$6766	$3886	$2953	$2508	$2255	$2098
$400 000	$7733	$4441	$3375	$2866	$2577	$2398
$450 000	$8700	$4996	$3797	$3224	$2899	$2698
$500 000	$9666	$5551	$4219	$3582	$3222	$2998
$550 000	$10 633	$6106	$4641	$3940	$3544	$3298
$600 000	$11 600	$6661	$5063	$4299	$3866	$3597
$650 000	$12 566	$7216	$5485	$4657	$4188	$3897
$700 000	$13 533	$7771	$5907	$5015	$4510	$4197
$750 000	$14 500	$8327	$6329	$5373	$4832	$4497

Loan	Years					
	5	10	15	20	25	30
$800 000	$15 466	$8882	$6751	$5731	$5154	$4796
$850 000	$16 433	$9437	$7173	$6090	$5477	$5096
$900 000	$17 400	$9992	$7595	$6448	$5799	$5396
$950 000	$18 366	$10 547	$8017	$6806	$6121	$5696
$1 000 000	$19 333	$11 102	$8439	$7164	$6443	$5996

For example, if you had a $650 000 home loan with $80 000 sitting in offset, your loan is equivalent to $570 000 ($650 000 − $80 000), so look at the $550 000 line (the line closest to your outstanding loan balance). If you were making $4500 monthly repayments off that loan, move along the $550 000 row until you find the number closest $4500, in this case $4641. With those figures, you'll pay off your outstanding loan in approximately 15 years at the current rate.

Once you know roughly how long it will take you to pay off your current loan, see how that compares with your plans to retire. Does the estimate of you paying off your loan line up with your desired time frame to retirement?

If the years remaining to repay your mortgage are longer than you are hoping to continue working, then you'll need to pay the loan off at a faster rate. You can use the table to work out what you'll need to repay each month to pay off your mortgage in your preferred timeline. Here's how:

■ Start with the row with the closest outstanding balance to your current mortgage.

■ Go across the columns to the column that lines up with your desired retirement time frame.

■ The number at the intersection of outstanding loan to years before retirement is what you need to be targeting.

If your mortgage is in excess of $1 million, you can still use this table to work out your repayments. Just add the numbers in the $1 million row with the remaining number. For example, if your loan is roughly $1.2 million add the $1 million row and the $200 000 rows together.

So you now know what it will take for you to repay your debts before you retire. What impact will this have on your net nest egg number? Look at the calculations you did in Chapter 2 for your net nest egg assets and take out any debts you had there. This will have the effect of increasing your net nest egg number. How far off are you from where you need to be to retire life ready?

Superannuation

The second key element (having enough money in other assets to support your retirement) is where things start to get a little more complicated. Most working Australians will have a solid starting base for their retirement because of the Australian superannuation system. I went into great detail about superannuation in Chapter 7, but given that superannuation was first introduced back in 1992, by now, most working Australians have had the benefit of forced, employer-paid retirement savings for the majority of their working lives.

Superannuation accumulated via default employer super contributions plus the age pension will be your safety net in retirement. It's from this we can build your more aspirational retirement.

What you now need to estimate is where your superannuation balance may be by the time you retire. Lots of superannuation funds have an estimation tool as part of their online services, but if you don't have access to one of those through your super fund, you could also use an online compound growth calculator (try moneysmart.gov.au/budgeting/compound-interest-calculator). The following tables will help you estimate your balance.

How to use these tables:

- Look at the table that most closely lines up with the years until your desired retirement.

- Look down the left column to find the starting balance that most closely lines up with your current superannuation balance.

- Go across the rows to the column that most closely lines up with your current annual rate of superannuation contributions.

- The intersection of your current approximate balance and your current rate of superannuation contributions will give you an estimate of what your superannuation balance may be in the future.

Five years until retirement

Starting balance	Annual contribution					
	$5000	$10000	$15000	$20000	$25000	$30000
$100000	$171016.12	$196702.81	$222389.49	$248076.17	$273762.86	$299449.54
$200000	$316345.56	$342032.25	$367718.93	$393405.61	$419092.30	$444778.98
$300000	$461675.01	$487361.69	$513048.37	$538735.06	$564421.74	$590108.42
$400000	$607004.45	$632691.13	$658377.81	$684064.50	$709751.18	$735437.86
$500000	$752333.89	$778020.57	$803707.25	$829393.94	$855080.62	$880767.30
$600000	$897663.33	$923350.01	$949036.69	$974723.38	$1000410.06	$1026096.74
$700000	$1042992.77	$1068679.45	$1094366.14	$1120052.82	$1145739.50	$1171426.18
$800000	$1188322.21	$1214008.89	$1239695.58	$1265382.26	$1291068.94	$1316755.63
$900000	$1333651.65	$1359338.33	$1385025.02	$1410711.70	$1436398.38	$1462085.07
$1000000	$1478981.09	$1504667.77	$1530354.46	$1556041.14	$1581727.82	$1607414.51

Ten years until retirement

Starting balance	Annual contribution					
	$5000	$10 000	$15 000	$20 000	$25 000	$30 000
$100 000	$274 223.46	$337 240.46	$400 257.45	$463 274.45	$526 291.44	$589 308.44
$200 000	$485 429.92	$548 446.92	$611 463.92	$674 480.91	$737 497.91	$800 514.90
$300 000	$696 636.39	$759 653.38	$822 670.38	$885 687.38	$948 704.37	$1 011 721.37
$400 000	$907 842.85	$970 859.85	$1 033 876.84	$1 096 893.84	$1 159 910.84	$1 222 927.83
$500 000	$1 119 049.31	$1 182 066.31	$1 245 083.31	$1 308 100.30	$1 371 117.30	$1 434 134.30
$600 000	$1 330 255.78	$1 393 272.77	$1 456 289.77	$1 519 306.77	$1 582 323.76	$1 645 340.76
$700 000	$1 541 462.24	$1 604 479.24	$1 667 496.23	$1 730 513.23	$1 793 530.23	$1 856 547.22
$800 000	$1 752 668.71	$1 815 685.70	$1 878 702.70	$1 941 719.69	$2 004 736.69	$2 067 753.69
$900 000	$1 963 875.17	$2 026 892.17	$2 089 909.16	$2 152 926.16	$2 215 943.15	$2 278 960.15
$1 000 000	$2 175 081.63	$2 238 098.63	$2 301 115.63	$2 364 132.62	$2 427 149.62	$2 490 166.61

231

Fifteen years until retirement

Starting balance	Annual contribution					
	$5000	$10000	$15000	$20000	$25000	$30000
$100000	$424214.10	$541483.04	$658751.97	$776020.90	$893289.83	$1010558.76
$200000	$731159.28	$848428.21	$965697.14	$1082966.07	$1200235.00	$1317503.93
$300000	$1038104.45	$1155373.38	$1272642.31	$1389911.24	$1507180.17	$1624449.11
$400000	$1345049.62	$1462318.55	$1579587.48	$1696856.42	$1814125.35	$1931394.28
$500000	$1651994.79	$1769263.73	$1886532.66	$2003801.59	$2121070.52	$2238339.45
$600000	$1958939.97	$2076208.90	$2193477.83	$2310746.76	$2428015.69	$2545284.62
$700000	$2265885.14	$2383154.07	$2500423.00	$2617691.93	$2734960.86	$2852229.80
$800000	$2572830.31	$2690099.24	$2807368.18	$2924637.11	$3041906.04	$3159174.97
$900000	$2879775.49	$2997044.42	$3114313.35	$3231582.28	$3348851.21	$3466120.14
$1000000	$3186720.66	$3303989.59	$3421258.52	$3538527.45	$3655796.38	$3773065.31

Twenty years until retirement

Starting balance	Annual contribution					
	$5000	$10000	$15000	$20000	$25000	$30000
$100000	$642194.67	$838307.63	$1034420.60	$1230533.56	$1426646.53	$1622759.49
$200000	$1088276.37	$1284389.34	$1480502.30	$1676615.27	$1872728.23	$2068841.20
$300000	$1534358.07	$1730471.04	$1926584.00	$2122696.97	$2318809.93	$2514922.90
$400000	$1980439.78	$2176552.74	$2372665.71	$2568778.67	$2764891.64	$2961004.60
$500000	$2426521.48	$2622634.45	$2818747.41	$3014860.38	$3210973.34	$3407086.31
$600000	$2872603.18	$3068716.15	$3264829.11	$3460942.08	$3657055.04	$3853168.01
$700000	$3318684.89	$3514797.85	$3710910.82	$3907023.78	$4103136.75	$4299249.71
$800000	$3764766.59	$3960879.56	$4156992.52	$4353105.49	$4549218.45	$4745331.42
$900000	$4210848.29	$4406961.26	$4603074.22	$4799187.19	$4995300.15	$5191413.12
$1000000	$4656930.00	$4853042.96	$5049155.93	$5245268.89	$5441381.86	$5637494.82

In constructing these tables, I've used 7.5 per cent as the annual return rate, which is pretty consistent with the long-term average returns on the balanced investment option from most superannuation providers. If you're in a growth or high-growth investment option, your long-term average return may be higher, and if you're in conservative investment option, it may be lower. Remember, these numbers are just a guide to see if you're headed in the right direction.

I'd encourage you to visit your super fund's website and look up the ten-year average return for the investment option your superannuation is in. Just remember, the returns your super fund earned over the last ten years are no guarantee of what it might earn for the next ten.

If you have a partner, repeat this estimate for their future superannuation balance with their rate of contributions and add it to yours. What does the total look like? Are you happy, surprised or sad?

How's your future looking?

So far you've tackled two steps towards building your net nest egg assets so you can retire life ready. You now have an:

- understanding of how long it will take you to repay your debt at your current repayment rate

- estimate of what your super balance may look like at retirement at your current contribution rate.

Now, with these two figures, can you see what difference this makes to your net nest egg assets at retirement? Let's revisit some of the tables from Chapter 2 so you can see what difference it makes.

Re-do your net nest egg asset calculation again, but this time include your estimated superannuation balance at retirement as well as the estimated outstanding balance of any loans at retirement. If your loans are looking like they will be repaid before your desired retirement age, even better—we'll deal with what to do with the money you were paying towards loans in Chapter 13.

Nest egg assets

Asset	Chapter 2 amount	New estimated amount
Cash/term deposit/offset account	$	
Combined super balances	$	
Investment property	$	
Shares/managed funds	$	
Business value	$	
TOTAL	$	

Debt

Liability	Chapter 2 amount	New estimated amount
Home loan	$	
Investment loan (property or shares)	$	
Car, boat, caravan loan	$	
Holiday home	$	
Superannuation debt	$	
Business debt	$	
TOTAL	$	

Net nest egg assets

Assets	Chapter 2 amount	New estimated amount
Total nest egg assets	$	
Less Liabilities		
Total debts	$	
Equals		
Net nest egg assets	$	

Your debts will have gone down (they might not be completely paid at your current rate, but you now know what you need to do so they will be paid), and your super balance will have grown.

Compare this updated net nest egg number to the numbers you needed using either the rule of 20x or the 4 per cent rule calculated in Chapter 3. Are you on track or do you still have a gap to close? If you still have a gap to close, that's okay, I'll cover some more steps to help you on page 247.

You've just completed a really important exercise in closing the gap. Not only do you understand where you need to get to (as you worked out in Chapter 3), you now have an idea of where you might end up just by paying down your debts and continuing to contribute to your superannuation fund. Without knowing where you might end up by just continuing to do what you are doing, you can't possibly know if you're heading in the right direction or if you have a really big job ahead of you to close the gap.

In my day job as a financial adviser, we have some tools we can use to help speed this part up rather than having to manually calculate things as you have just done. When I work through these two elements with clients, they are often surprised how close they get to their retirement number by doing nothing more than working, continuing to pay down their debts and collecting superannuation.

Were you just as surprised?

What I like to do is set this as the baseline of what's achievable without doing anything more than you are currently doing today, other than staying healthy enough so you can continue to work.

Remember, we haven't yet spoken about allocating any of that difference between what you earn and what you spend just yet. We'll get to that next.

Retire life ready steps

You covered some big exercises in this chapter, and some of them may have felt confronting while others perhaps left you with a sense of comfort that you are on the right track.

Which part of this did you feel most confident in?

Maybe you found that you could pay off your mortgage quicker than anticipated? Or perhaps (like many people I speak with) you were pleasantly surprised by how much super you might have at retirement?

Which part did you find the most challenging? Where did you identify the biggest gap in your current financial trajectory? Wherever that was, the next section will help you to work on that.

CHAPTER 13
Allocating your surplus

In Chapter 2, you identified the difference between what you earn and what you spend. In financial planning, we call this your *surplus income*. This is money that you can choose to allocate to other areas to make that money work harder and grow more surplus. Ultimately, this is money you can take and use to grow more money or pay off debts faster! It's money you can invest in your dream lifestyle, both now and in the future.

As much as this book is about retiring life ready, between now and retirement, there will be other things you want to achieve. For example, in Chapter 4, I introduced you to a couple who put a lot of short-term focus on family holidays before their children got too old and didn't want to go with them anymore.

If you have other priorities between now and retirement (holidays is a big one for most people I speak with), it's important that you allocate some of this surplus towards those things. I don't like to see people give up everything now in the hope of a better retirement; you need to enjoy the present too.

After you've allocated some money towards your shorter term goals and activities, it's time to see what impact the difference can make to paying off your debts and/or boosting your super.

Extra super contributions

Should you put more into your mortgage or make extra super contributions? This would have to be one of the most common retirement planning questions I get.

If you have space up to your concessional contribution cap (see Chapter 7 for an explanation), the maths says more into super is the better option, and the reason the maths says it's a better option is all to do with the tax savings on super-annuation contributions.

If you can contribute extra to superannuation as a concessional contribution, you only pay 15 per cent tax on that contribution (or 30 per cent if you earn over $250000), which is a far lower rate of tax than what most people pay on their income from work. As a result of paying less tax by contributing that money to super, you have more money available to you to invest in your super fund than you would have had available to make extra loan repayments. On top of the tax savings that money invested in your superannuation fund will have earned, you'll also receive a higher long-term average return than the interest cost on your mortgage.

To work out how much you could afford to salary sacrifice to superannuation (as pre-tax concessional contributions), you need to divide your monthly surplus by 1 minus your marginal tax rate. Let me explain with an example (and feel free to substitute these numbers with your own real-life examples).

Case study: Using surplus income to boost super

Meet our fictional couple Stuart and Monica. They want to use their surplus income to boost their super.

Stuart and Monica worked through the exercises in Chapter 2 and discovered they have $1500 per month surplus income. Stuart and Monica are both 50, and are planning to retire around 60, but would work a little longer if they needed to so that they can afford the retirement they aspire to.

Stuart earns $90000 and Monica $170000, and their employers pay superannuation on top of those salaries at the government-mandated rate of 12 per cent, which means Stuart receives $10800 in concessional superannuation contributions from his employer, and Monica receives $20400 from hers.

	Stuart	Monica
Income	$90000	$170000
Annual concessional contribution cap (a)	$30000	$30000
Employer super contributions (b)	$10800	$20400
Unused concessional contribution cap (a – b)	$19200	$9600
Marginal tax rate	30%*	37%*

* Plus 2 per cent Medicare

Monica and Stuart could allocate their $1500 per month surplus to additional superannuation contributions or extra

(continued)

loan repayments. If we look at using that money to make additional concessional (pre-tax) super contributions, we need to work out what their $1500 monthly surplus equates to as pre-tax dollars.

Here's how you do it:

Monthly surplus
1 – marginal tax rate
= pre-tax monthly surplus

If we said all of that surplus came from Monica's income, it looks like:

$1500
1 – 39%
= $2459

You'll notice Stuart and Monica have different marginal tax rates because of their different incomes. They will each have a different pre-tax monthly surplus if you allocate all the surplus to one person versus the other. In this case, we'll need to do the calculation twice.

For Monica, the pre-tax monthly surplus equates to $2459.

Let's look at how that equation works for Stuart's income:

$1500
1 – 32%
= $2205

For Stuart, the pre-tax monthly surplus equates to $2205.

Monica could contribute $2459 per month, or $29508 per annum, to super as concessional contributions, and this would use up all of their $1500 per month surplus. But, as per the example in the table, Monica only has $9600 available in unused concessional contributions because her employer is already contributing $20400 for her, and the concessional contribution cap is currently $30000 (ignoring any carry forward allowance she may have; more on that in Chapter 7). If Monica uses up all of her available cap, Stuart could use the balance of their surplus income to contribute to his superannuation fund.

Monica makes an additional $9600 per annum in super contributions, less the 15 per cent tax on concessional superannuation contributions, and her account will be credited with an additional $8160. Stuart contributes the balance of their surplus cash flow, which equates to $17858 before tax at Stuart's marginal tax rate. If we subtract the 15 per cent contributions tax payable on concessional superannuation contributions, this becomes $15170.30.

Plug these additional contributions into a compound growth calculator at an assumed earnings rate of 7.5 per cent, and you can estimate that they would have an additional $347000 in super over the next ten years. This could be the difference between them getting to their net nest egg asset target or not. This additional $347000 would equate to approximately $15000 per annum more spending income in retirement—that's another holiday or an upgrade to an existing one!

Using the same formula (and the estimated super balance tables in Chapter 12), what could your super contributions look like if you allocated some or all of your monthly surplus? What does this additional contribution do to your projected super balance over the next, five, 10, 20 years?

Extra debt repayments

In Chapter 12, I asked you to work out how long it would take you to pay off your debts if you just kept making repayments as you currently are. If it was looking like you wouldn't have your debts paid before retirement at your current repayment rate, I now want you to work out what difference it would make to your retirement position if you allocated some of your surplus income to making extra debt repayments.

Using the mortgage calculator on page 62, see what your debt repayment schedule would look like if you increased your monthly payments using your surplus. What number would most closely align with your retire life ready timeline? Put the estimates in the following table.

	How long to pay off your loans?
Repaying debts at current rate	
Adding surplus to make extra debt repayments	

Case study: Increasing loan repayments

Let's revisit Stuart and Monica.

Stuart and Monica have been in their home for a number of years and have an outstanding mortgage on their home of $450 000. They currently make repayments of $3800 per month, which, at their current interest rate of 6.1 per cent, will see them pay off their home loan in around 15 years. They are hoping to be retired in ten years (if they can), so something needs to change.

If they increased their loan repayments by the surplus $1500 per month they have available, they would then be making loan repayments of $5300 per month. The increased repayments would see them pay off their loan in a little over nine years, which lines up with retirement in ten years quite nicely.

Once the mortgage is gone, they can then direct the $5300 per month they were making in mortgage repayments (current repayment + surplus) into investments to help fund their retirement.

Extra super or extra loan repayments?

So the maths says salary sacrificing to super is the better option, but there are two key differences between the two that you need to understand.

1. Additional repayments on a home loan is a guaranteed, risk-free return. Additional superannuation contributions are not.

2. Extra repayments you make to your home loan are often accessible if you need that money for some reason via your redraw account. You generally can't access money from your super fund until you've turned 60.

The guaranteed return from extra loan repayments comes in the form of interest saved on your home loan. You know what the interest rate on your home loan is; by paying extra off your home loan, you know exactly how much interest it will save you — there's no variability in that (other than your mortgage rate moving up or down), and you can't ever get a negative return (the interest saved is always a positive outcome).

On the other hand, the superannuation contributions have a guaranteed saving on tax (the tax rate on the super contributions is lower than what you pay on your salary), but that's where the guarantee for extra superannuation contributions ends.

The investment return on your superannuation fund is not guaranteed. You will have some years of great returns and some years of poor returns (with the odd negative). You need to have the investment appetite and the time horizon to ride out the ups and downs that result in superannuation being the best option mathematically.

Your own attitude also needs to be considered in this. Some people are happy to carry the home loan debt for a while longer in the hope of a better financial outcome from making additional superannuation contributions; others really dislike having debt and so paying it off as quickly as possible is the better option for them.

Case study: Deciding where to allocate a surplus

Let's revisit the two outcomes for Monica and Stuart.

By making additional contributions to superannuation, it's estimated that Monica and Stuart could increase their combined superannuation balance by $347000 over ten years. It's easy to look at the $347000 and say that's less than the $450000 home loan they paid off in the same period as a result of making extra loan repayments, so paying off the mortgage is the way to go. That's not quite the way to look at it.

Remember, Monica and Stuart are still paying off their $450000 mortgage at $3800 per month. It's just the extra $1500 per month surplus they haven't directed to their mortgage, which is going to superannuation contributions instead.

As a result of not making the extra loan repayments, they will still have an outstanding mortgage of approximately $200 000 in ten years' time when they plan to retire. They could withdraw $200 000 from their superannuation funds (tax free) after retiring at age 60 and pay out their remaining mortgage that way.

In this example, the contributions to superannuation (instead of paying off the mortgage faster) result in an extra approximately $147 000 to help fund their retirement: the extra $347 000 in superannuation (as a result of the extra contributions over ten years) less the $200 000 mortgage outstanding at age 60.

The simple path

Before we look at other forms of investing, and ways to build your wealth as you head towards retirement, let's just round out what can be a really simple path to retirement and may very well suit a lot of people.

If you're not interested in lavish overseas trips — maybe just one or two of those might do you — and you have a modest mortgage, your retirement planning may not need to be overly complicated. I really like the idea of taking the stress out of retirement planning and not making things unnecessarily complicated.

If you don't have a big gap you need to work on closing, paying down your home mortgage (and any other debt you may have) before retirement and working in a job where you collect some good super contributions may very well be enough for you to reach your net nest egg assets number.

Retire life ready steps

In the last part of this chapter, you looked at the impact on your loan balances, after directing any surplus income towards repayments. You also looked at the increase in your super balance by directing any surplus income towards extra super contributions. I'd encourage you to re-calculate your retirement net nest egg asset number using the:

- reduced outstanding loan balances you calculated

- increased super balance you calculated as a result of extra superannuation contributions.

How's it looking? Hopefully by now the gap isn't looking quite as scary it was in the beginning.

For most people, there is still a gap after allowing for either of these two basic paths. That's what we'll tackle next.

CHAPTER 14
A step beyond the basics

For a lot of people, just working and paying off their home loan or adding some extra money to their super still isn't going to enable them to retire and enjoy the lifestyle they are aiming for. Sometimes that is because they have some really big aspirations when it comes to their retirement income goals or retirement lifestyle, and other times, they've left things a little too late on the investing front.

I work with some couples who want to be able to spend $300000 or $500000 or even more per annum after tax in retirement. These are often owners and operators of quite successful businesses that have paid them significant salaries over an extended period. As a result, they have become accustomed to a particular lifestyle (maintaining multiple homes, multiple cars and regular overseas trips) that they don't want to give up in retirement.

Because of the somewhat restrictive contribution limits and eventual caps on superannuation balances, for those with bigger retirement income targets, we're going to have to look further than just paying down a mortgage and topping up super. Adding lots of money to superannuation also isn't a great idea if your goal is to retire from work earlier than age 60 when you can access your super. Having most of your money in super is great in that scenario, but having all of your money in super isn't.

Generally, when someone has big retirement targets, they have done a fair amount of work in building their assets before I get involved; however, sometimes a client's goals and the reality of those goals are at odds with each other.

Some clients might be able to save and invest an amount of money towards paying down their debts or topping up super, but it might not be enough. Then I have to have the somewhat difficult conversation with them to explain something has to give — they either need to work longer to afford the retirement they want, they need to sacrifice more today so they can invest more for later, or they have to accept a lesser retirement income than what they were hoping for. There's no magic answer, just a level of compromise.

It's not my job to tell them which option to choose; it's my job to alert them to the issue, give them some options and let them choose. Then, once they have made their choice, support them in making the best financial decisions that align with this new direction.

Investing outside of superannuation

Your accumulated superannuation balance will likely cover the majority of your retirement income needs, particularly if you've actively contributed more than just the default employer contributions for at least ten to 15 years prior to retirement. But, for some, it won't be enough. For some, their retirement spending number is so high that superannuation alone won't be enough. For others, they have left contributing to superannuation too late, and while they have the means to contribute more to superannuation, the annual caps get in the way.

Superannuation works best if you add more than your employer contributions, for a *long* time. I'm talking 20 years or more if you can. Don't leave it until the last five years before you retire.

The higher your desired retirement spending number, the more you will need to be able to contribute towards your investing and paying down debt, and the earlier you need to get started. There are no free rides here, no get-rich-quick schemes — it's much more get rich slow.

So you're actively paying down your debt, adding more to your superannuation and you still have the means to do more — and you need to because you're aspiring to an amazing retirement. This is where some of the structuring elements I discussed through Part II of this book come into play.

Decide what to invest in first

You first need to decide on your desired investment asset, which is really going to be a decision between investing in the stock market (outside of your superannuation) or buying an investment property. Both of these options have their pros and cons, which I discussed in Chapter 5.

When we reach this part of the journey with clients I'm providing financial advice to, the majority of people will definitely say they want to invest in property or they want to invest in shares. Only a small number are indifferent. Those who say 'property' often add something about it being 'less risky' (which it isn't), and the fact that they are comfortable borrowing money for investment purposes and like the idea of negative-gearing tax breaks. Those who say they want to invest in the share market often aren't comfortable with the idea of borrowing money for investment purposes, nor do they want to deal with the headaches that can arise from being a landlord.

Shares or property?

As mentioned previously, shares and property each have their own pros and cons. Your decision will come down to personal preference and affordability.

Property costs a lot to purchase initially and will have an ongoing commitment from you to maintain the mortgage. You're unlikely to be investing in a property where the rental income covers the entirety of the loan repayments; you'll have to contribute something yourself, and there's no getting out of that commitment until the loan is repaid or you sell the property.

While this ongoing commitment can put pressure on your finances from time to time, the leverage you take on (borrowing money to purchase the property) means that, provided you purchased an investment property that grows in value, you are highly likely to end up in a greater asset position by investing in property than you are by investing in shares. That doesn't mean it's the 'right' investment for you though. Given property is so costly to purchase in the first place and then later sell, you'll want to be able to hold the property for at least ten years before retirement so you have the best chance of profiting from the investment.

Your time frame to retirement plays a big part in the appropriateness of shares versus property for this part of your wealth-building activities. While investing in shares would typically require the same time horizon that I just mentioned for property, the ease at which you can buy (and sell, if need be) shares at far lower costs than property tends to lend itself to a shorter duration than a property investment.

How do the returns look?

According to research from CoreLogic, nationally, dwelling values have increased at an annual compounding rate of 5.4 per cent for the 30 years to August 2022. Add on top of that the rental income you earn, and the average return from property is almost identical to the average return from the share market. But let me show you the difference leverage makes with another example.

Case study: The value of long-term property investment

Meet Paul. Paul owns his own home and is already contributing extra towards his superannuation and paying down his home loan. The additional repayments he's been making towards his home loan means he has accessible equity (the difference between the value of his home and the outstanding loan) that he could borrow for a deposit on an investment property.

(continued)

Paul also has $2000 monthly surplus income, over and above what he is already contributing to superannuation, that he can use for investment purposes.

Paul purchases an $800000 investment property by borrowing some money secured against his house (called releasing equity), and borrows some further money secured against the new investment property to finalise the purchase and cover purchase costs. All up, he borrows $850000.

Paul gets a tenant into the property who pays him market rent and Paul's $2000 per month surplus income goes towards helping to pay the shortfall on the mortgage between the payments due and the rent received, as well as the other costs associated with holding a property.

At a compound growth rate of 5.4 per cent, this is how the value of Paul's investment property increases:

Purchase price	$800000
Year 1	$843200
Year 5	$1040622
Year 10	$1353618
Year 15	$1760756
Year 20	$2290352
Year 25	$2979238
Year 30	$3875327

If Paul had an interest-only loan for 20 years (not likely to be possible, but go with me), his net equity position at the end of 20 years would be $1440352 ($2290352–$850000). An even better scenario is if Paul paid off the loan over the 20 years, in which case his equity position would be the full value of the investment property $2290352.

Notice how rapidly the value of the property increases towards the end of the 30 years compared with the beginning? This is the power of compounding and reinforces the idea of starting on this journey as early as you can.

Shares, on the other hand, are a whole lot easier to get started with. Rather than invest all in one go as you tend to do with property, you start small and build your balance slowly. While it's possible to borrow money for investing in the share market, and plenty of people have done so quite successfully, it's certainly not the starting position for most people like it is with property.

Comparing a shares scenario to property

If, instead of buying the investment property, Paul invested the $2000 per month into a diversified share market investment and earned the same 7.5 per cent average return we used in Chapter 13, then he would build an investment portfolio of $110746. It's a lot of money, but not quite as much as the property built over the same time period.

If Paul didn't pay off the $850000 loan, eventually, the share portfolio would catch the equity in the investment property and overtake it. But, on the numbers used here, that would take 37 years. If Paul was also paying down the investment property debt over time, the share portfolio would not likely catch the property value in Paul's lifetime.

So which should you choose?

It would be easy to jump to the conclusion that because the property investment provided the better outcome over 20 years, based on the return assumptions used here, that's the way you should go.

But that's not the way I'd encourage you to look at it. Instead, look at what you need to build your net nest egg number to so that you can achieve your desired spending number and live your retired life the way you design it.

More money for the sake of more money is pointless. You need a purpose, your money needs a purpose, and that purpose will give you direction. You need to build your plans around what you need to achieve to get to where you need to get to.

As you worked through the revisions to your net nest egg number, paying down debt and estimating where your superannuation balance may get to, perhaps you were only a small way off the net nest egg number you need to support your spending number. If that's the case, you likely don't need to take on the risk of borrowing money and all the costs associated with buying an investment property. Perhaps with a regular investment into the share market, you can build enough of an additional portfolio to get to where you need to be.

Or, perhaps, your net nest egg number, after paying down your debts and estimating your superannuation balance, is so far off where you need to be that you do need to take on the risk of borrowing money and buying an investment property. Perhaps you need to buy multiple. If you are heading down this route, tread carefully — the more debt you take on, the more risk you are adding to your strategy. If it pays off, it will likely pay off handsomely for you. If it doesn't pay off, you'll be in a lot of financial trouble with likely not many years left to try and fix the situation.

As I explain to clients, I like to see you build the assets you need to build to support the life you want to lead with the least amount of risk possible. More money for the sake of more money is pointless in my view and just adds unnecessary risk to your plans.

Determine your structure

Once you've decided on what you need to or are comfortable investing in, the last thing you need to decide is how you're going to own the asset. Through Part II of this book, I described a number of structures you can use to do this, such as investing under individual names or through a trust, and each has its place for the right person at the right time.

When it comes to working out what ownership structure you might use, it's best to start with the end in mind. If the assets you're purchasing outside of the superannuation environment will eventually be sold to help pay down debt and/or fund your retirement, think about which structure might provide you with the best capital gains tax outcome at the end. If you intend to hold the assets as income to fund your retirement, think about how you might pay the least amount of tax on that income through your retirement years.

Don't just go buying negatively geared investment properties in the highest income earner's name because, as you pay down debts associated with the property, it won't be negatively geared anymore and the investment income will be taxed at the higher income earner's rate. If you sell the property while the owner is still working, you'll have capital gains tax to pay on top of that person's ordinary income.

If you are part of a couple and one person earns considerably less than the other, consider buying investments in the lower income earner's name to benefit from lower marginal tax rates. Or, if one of you plan on retiring before the other, maybe a trust might be a good idea so from one year to the next you can decide who gets distributed the trust income to pay tax on.

If you're a single person, owning assets in someone else's name isn't an option for you, so perhaps buying assets in a trust so you can distribute any income to a company (refer to page 188) may be the way to go. Or if you're going to invest in the share market, perhaps establishing an investment bond might be the simpler and easier way to get that share market exposure.

Getting this part right helps you keep more of your hard-earned investments, which puts you that little bit closer to retiring life ready.

Retire life ready steps

Do you need to do more than just pay off your debts and top-up your super to meet your retirement goals?

What amount of regular (surplus) income do you have to put towards the additional investing? $_____

List the additional investment options you are going to explore:

_____

_____

_____

_____

CHAPTER 15
From accumulating to living

Congratulations on making it this far! We now need to tackle the final element of retiring life ready — managing the transition from accumulating assets so that you have enough to support your dream retirement to living off what you've built.

It is highly unlikely that the assets you have accumulated up until your retirement will be the same assets that take you through retirement. This is something I explain to new clients regularly.

Once you retire life ready, the focus shifts from building your asset base to those assets supporting the dream retirement you outlined back in Chapter 1. To recap, the two main phases look like this:

1. Accumulation: During this stage you have a strong focus on growth through things such as topping up your super,

buying an investment property, investing in the share market and paying down your debt. Your income from investments isn't really necessary as you're still working. The income you earn from work covers your lifestyle and the income from investments is fully taxable at (up to) marginal tax rates, so you don't really want much of it if you're being smart with your tax planning. Growth is what you are chasing.

2. Living from investments: In this stage, the income from work stops, so you need to replace that with income from investments. Growth, while still important so that you can live a long, happy retirement and combat inflation, takes a back seat to income from your investments and your ability to get your hands on cash for spending. Now those properties, with all the debt you were negatively gearing, are holding you back from retiring, and having your super in the high-growth investment option, holding a big share portfolio and not having much in cash aren't such great ideas anymore.

As you head into the final couple of years of your working life, you need to start planning how you will move from the accumulating stage to the living off your assets stage. What assets do you need to sell, what investment debt do you need to clear, and how will you rebalance your superannuation and share investments so you can retire when you are ready to and access the cash you need on day one of your retirement?

Day one of retirement — what a day that will be. I'd really love it if you sent me a message on Instagram (@iamjameswrigley) and told me what you did on day one of your retirement.

Now let's work through the most common transitions from your working life to your dream retirement life you'll need to deal with so that you can plan for them appropriately.

When to retire?

When in the financial year is the best time to retire? Some people are fit and healthy and this is a choice they get to make. Others, unfortunately, don't get that choice, perhaps due to poor health or an unplanned redundancy late in their working life when finding a new job becomes increasingly difficult (anyone who's tried to find a new job on the wrong side of 55 will know this feeling).

If you do have the choice, the absolute best thing you can do is use up your leave entitlements before you stop working. If you've got some long service leave owing, for example, use that leave up before you retire. If you use your leave, rather than have it paid out, you collect further leave as well as superannuation contributions. Using your leave can mean many thousands of dollars in additional benefits to you versus having all your entitlements paid out.

If you do retire and have your leave paid out to you in one go, the best thing you can do is retire early in a new financial year. This way, any entitlements you do receive aren't added on top of a full year's salary and taxed at a potentially higher rate. You will, no doubt, have some tax deducted from your entitlements being paid out (even if you're paid in a new financial year), but if you don't have a whole lot of other income in that same financial year, you may get most of the tax refunded back to you at tax time.

Maximising property after retirement

I'm always interested in why people choose to invest in property and what their plans for those properties are come retirement. In Chapter 14, we looked at how, at least mathematically, your ability to borrow a lot of money to buy property can magnify your investing gains dramatically if you get the property investment right.

Often, though, the reason people have accumulated investment properties as part of their plans come retirement is a lot simpler than that. They simply plan to hold the properties and use the rental income to fund their retirement — that is, until they realise (or it's pointed out to them) how little spending money they actually have from the rent they earn.

While you earn rental income, you also have rental expenses. Those expenses don't stop when you retire and they eat into your cash flow. Unless you have millions and millions of dollars worth of (paid-off) investment properties heading into retirement, and you plan to live a modest retirement, your investment properties will likely need to be sold at some point.

So, when do you sell? Putting aside the 'right' time from a market valuation perspective, because I have no particular insights worth sharing there, if we just focus on the tax implications of selling property to better fund retirement, then it's easier to make some decisions.

First, assuming you've made good gains on the investment property, you, ideally, don't want to sell it until the next financial year following your retirement. Say, for example, you retired in July and had any leave entitlements or a redundancy package paid early in one financial year, you might want to wait until the following financial year to sell the investment property. As I explained in Chapter 6, any gains you make from selling investments are added on top of your ordinary income and taxed at marginal tax rates (less a 50 per cent discount for assets held for more than 12 months), so selling in a financial year following your retirement will likely mean less capital gains tax to pay.

What you need to balance there is your age and whether you will be young enough to use concessional contributions to superannuation to help reduce your capital gains tax bill further. Be careful of turning 67 and losing access to making concessional contributions without needing to satisfy the work test (refer back Chapter 7 on Superannuation).

Client story: Million-dollar properties

I'm doing some work for a client who has, by any metric, been a very successful property investor. Between their home and investment properties, they own eight properties worth in excess of $15 million. There's around $5 million in debts across those properties, but even at that level, without working, they can't afford to hold all the properties as they are cash flow negative. We are mapping out plans to progressively sell the properties and pay off their debts.

The plan is to sell one each financial year (to help reduce capital gains tax) until all their debts are paid and they can live off the rental income from the properties they don't sell. But, even then, the properties they retain won't be enough to cover the $250 000 retirement income they want to live off, so they will need to top-up the rent they receive with superannuation pensions. That will fund their retirement

(continued)

for many years, but depending on their spending patterns later in retirement and the rental income growth over time, they may need to sell the remaining investment properties so they can keep funding their retirement.

How to structure your superannuation for retirement

If you've been following some version of the three-bucket approach (flick back to page 98 for a refresher) to managing your investments, you probably have your superannuation invested into a high-growth investment option with your superannuation provider. Or, if you've moved to a superannuation structure where you have even more control, it's likely all your superannuation is 'invested' with very little in cash. This isn't an ideal set-up on the day you retire.

It's not ideal to be 100 per cent growth or in high growth on the day you retire, nor is it great to leave it until the day you retire to rebalance your superannuation to something more appropriate for your retirement years.

What matters for your superannuation is when you plan on accessing your benefits, not necessarily when you plan on retiring. Take the extreme of someone who retires at 50 because they have accumulated enough wealth to be able to do so. That 50-year-old can't access their superannuation benefits for another ten years (at age 60), so switching to a more conservative investment option at retirement (50) isn't such a great idea for them. They would be better off maximising their investments until closer to their retirement.

What I like to see is someone starting to transition out of the 'all growth' allocation around two to three years out from when they plan on accessing their superannuation. Taking it a step further, if you've taken real control of how your superannuation is invested, I wouldn't want to see you sell out of your growth investments, rather, I'd prefer you to just stop buying more of those investments.

If you're following the three-bucket investment approach, bucket 3 will be generating income from the investments you own. Rather than using that income to buy more investments as you may have done up until this point, I like to see that income being used to build out buckets 1 and 2. Further, as you continue contributing to your super for those last few years of your working life, use those contributions to build out buckets 1 and 2 as well. Stop buying more growth investments with your contributions and income from investments, and instead build up your cash-type holdings.

If you manage the transition of your superannuation this way, you can slowly move from a 'growth' profile to a 'balanced' profile without actually selling anything. If you're not selling anything, you don't have to pay capital gains tax, but bigger than that, you don't have to worry about finding the 'right' time to sell your growth investments or be too exposed to a downturn in markets during the last year of your working life.

Using your share portfolio to support your retirement

Much the same as the discussion around transitioning your superannuation to be ready to fund your retirement, if you're going to be relying on your share portfolio to support part of your retirement income needs, you'll want to go through a similar transition with your share portfolio.

Looking at your share portfolio, the first step would be to ensure you have money in buckets 1 and 2. So, like super, use the dividends from your shares to build those buckets up, and any money you may have been dollar cost averaging (see page 95) into shares, direct that to bucket 1- and 2-type investments instead.

Like the discussion on property, you should take a look at the individual investments you are holding. Are those shares dividend payers? Do you have some paying franking credits that can help reduce your tax bill or, even better, be refunded back to you at tax time so you've got additional income? Do you have some that will continue to grow in value to help combat inflation over time?

Depending on the structure through which you hold those shares, you'll also need to manage the tax implications of any shares you choose to sell as you head into retirement. If you own them in your own name, you might not want to make any major changes until the financial year after you've retired to minimise capital gains tax implications. Alternatively, you might have them in some other structure where capital gains tax isn't quite the same problem.

Your debt has to go

Then, finally, your debt has to go. All of it. Gone. If you haven't managed to pay off your debts by the time you retire, it has to go.

You absolutely cannot be heading into retirement with outstanding debt on your home. Sell some investments, draw on your superannuation or downsize — do whatever you need to do to get rid of the mortgage on your own home. You will feel so much freer.

Debt on investments is only just, and I mean just, acceptable, but it has to go shortly after retirement. It's hard enough to build the assets you need to generate the income required to cover your lifestyle, let alone try and have extra to continue to pay these debts. They need to go.

Forget the negative gearing benefits of the debt on your investment property. Those benefits are useless when you are retired and you have no income from work to offset those losses against — they are just making it harder for you to fund retirement.

For many, this is the first time in their adult life they haven't had a debt to pay — enjoy it, you've earned it.

You're now set to retire life ready.

Retire life ready steps

Back in Chapter 4, you listed all your debts. Let's flick back to page 29 and have another look at them now.

In Chapter 12, you did some work trying to understand what your debts might look like at retirement if you kept paying them off as you were, then in Chapter 13, you did some further work to understand what those debts might look like if you allocated some surplus income towards them.

What does that new debt position look like at your ideal retirement age?

Do you need to prioritise paying off more debt? Or will you have the assets you can sell to repay the debt in retirement?

I'd encourage you to map out a plan about how you intend to transition from accumulation to living off your wealth — include things such as selling investment properties or other investments (if you need to), transitioning your superannuation fund from high-growth to a more retirement-friendly mix. When will you start to access your super? If you're planning to retire before age 60, what will you live off before you can access your super?

What does five years out from retirement look like?

What does three years out from retirement look like?

What does one year out from retirement look like?

PUTTING IT ALL TOGETHER

Ideas without action are meaningless. Setting off on a journey without a destination in mind makes it impossible to know whether you should turn left or right at the end of the street, and the same applies to how you approach your ideal retirement.

During your journey to retire life ready, your destination may change, but I hope I've given you a roadmap you can follow through this book. If along that journey, your destination changes, pick up the book and revisit these steps to help guide you towards your new destination.

Step 1: Design your ideal retirement

Start by designing the retirement you aspire to. Don't settle for the one you end up with. While you have some time ahead of you, now is the time to write down all your big goals and aspirations. What do you really want to do, where do you want to go and who can help you get there?

Step 2: Look at what you have now

Take stock of where you are now, where you are starting from. Look at what you own versus what you owe: remember, it's common to be starting from a negative position when you exclude the value of your home from your asset pool.

Armed with this knowledge and by exerting control over what you earn and what you spend, you can turn that negative into a positive and be well onto the path to where you need to be.

Step 3: Work out your spending number

Given the retirement you are aspiring to, work out what it's going to cost you. I introduced the idea of your spending number on page 27. Start with what you might spend each year, then work back to the net investment assets you need to support that income using either the rule of 20x or the 4 per cent rule.

You now know where you need to get to, why you want to get there and where you're starting from.

Step 4: Get your house in order

Use the various building blocks available to you: save, invest, pay down debt, manage your tax as best you can, protect your ability to earn an income, understand how inheritance impacts you, and help loved ones manage their later years through the aged care system.

It sounds like a lot when I list it like that, but take Part II of this book one chapter at a time. Implement some changes as you go, and remember, not everyone needs every single thing in Part II. Keep your plans as simple as you possibly can to get you to where you need to get to.

Step 5: Close the gap

Time, more than anything, is your friend here. The sooner you start working on closing the gap, the easier it is, the smaller the regular financial commitment it takes and the less risk you need to take on.

Once you've arrived at your destination, review whether the mix of assets that got you there are the same ones that will take you through retirement. If you do need to move things around for a better retirement, plan it out to minimise the taxes you might pay at this stage.

• • •

That's it, you've finished.

Thanks again for picking up this book, I do hope you've found it helpful. If you want to continue learning, feel free to follow me on either Instagram, TikTok, Facebook or LinkedIn.

You can also join the Retire Life Ready community in the Facebook group. I'd love to hear your comments on the book in there.

All the best,

James Wrigley

Instagram and TikTok: @iamjameswrigley
Facebook: facebook.com/jameswrigleyadviser
LinkedIn: linkedin.com/in/james-wrigley

RESOURCES

Your retire life ready journey has just begun and the information in this book is a stepping stone to launch you in the right direction for future financial security. If you want to find out more, here are some resources that I regularly recommend to clients.

- Book resources and other material: jameswrigley.com.au

- Finance calculators, retirement planners and compound growth calculators: moneysmart.gov.au

- Work out your tax payable and after-tax income: paycalculator.com.au

- Work out how long your mortgage will take to be paid off: mortgage.monster

- Current information on the age pension and health care cards: servicesaustralia.gov.au

- Aged care information and estimating costs: myagedcare.gov.au.

INDEX

12 301

Printed and bound by CPI Group (UK) Ltd, Croydon, CR0 4YY

22/10/2025

14749190-0001